THE
LOVED
ONES

— ESSAYS TO BURY THE DEAD —

MADISON DAVIS

DZANC
BOOKS

2580 Craig Rd.
Ann Arbor, MI 48103
www.dzancbooks.org

Library of Congress Cataloguing-in-Publication Data Available Upon Request

First Edition: June 2023
Cover design by Steven Seighman
Interior design byMichelle Dotter
ISBN: 9781950539772

Printed in the United States of America

10   9   8   7   6   5   4   3   2   1

contents

kill me good

These executions will be a perfect tonic for the entire division. There are few things more fundamentally encouraging and stimulating than seeing someone else die.

—Paths of Glory

IF YOU DRIVE EAST FROM Raymond, Washington, up Highway 101 and take a left just before a big sign welcomes you to the town of South Bend and you wind around into the green hills for a few miles and you take the right unmarked dirt road which branches off into the thick woods, you'll find a little cemetery. It was created by the Independent Order of Odd Fellows along with other fraternal organizations in the area in the late 1800s. It is known locally only as "Odd Fellows," which can be seen as a beautifully apt reference to the occupants of all cemeteries who are, by definition, the odd people out of living society.

It's maintained at the center—the grass is still occasionally mowed between the misshapen rows—but if you walk a bit farther, you'll find the surrounding woods are consuming it at the edges. It's difficult to tell now where the original boundary would have been. Gravestones are wrapped in tree roots and peek out above the spongy moss covering the forest floor. There is the grave of a child marked only with a decaying wood crib set against a rich oak tree, at once both protecting and swallowing it. There are granite markers eroded and reclaimed, rotting away in tandem with the bodies below them. It's a place where the earth has gently, but powerfully, overwritten our sense of death and life as being experienced by an individual. It's where human desire to memorialize the dead meets nature's ambivalence toward that need.

I find the idea of my dead body being placed there—slowly dissolving nestled into the soft moss and woven root structures—a deeply comforting one. Those who need to eat could eat. Those who need to mourn could mourn. Something could grow there.

QUIET EXCEPTIONS: These are not my bones.

IN THE FIERCE FEBRUARY COLD of Spokane, Washington, it was hard to imagine there could be such a thing as fire; hard to imagine the winter would allow it. But there I was in front of a small house, half in ashes and half still standing in the blistering cold. The house itself looked contagious. It looked like evidence. It looked like a place to run from, but I don't remember wanting to run. It was my family falling into the pit. My blood narrative spilled in this home. I wanted to get closer.

The windows were boarded with large pieces of plywood. A soft grey leaked out of the edges like slept-in mascara. From the sidewalk, my eyes followed footprints in the grass crisscrossing the front yard. A dewy frozen map of the events. Something to decode. The dull noise of the highway and strip mall just over the fence to my left was a steady atmospheric hum. I should have been on a distant planet.

But as I write this now, I'm not sure about the footprints. The timeline doesn't add up. I stood on that sidewalk days after it happened. Could those traces still have lingered in the yard? If not, why do I recall them so vividly? Why would I make it up?

What I can remember, unmistakably, is feeling as though if I listened hard enough, I should still be able to hear it. Somewhere just under the present was the unquenchable echo of screams and flames and firefighters and police and reporters still existing in an altogether different kind of time. Time had collapsed—all events being suddenly layered, as death has a way of doing—and the footprints, or the memory of the footprints, helped me understand the feeling that I was gliding uncontrollably between genera of time that had suddenly become distinct. They held me to a linear march of events. They divided yesterday from today. They helped me hold the incongruency of what cannot happen verging into what has happened.

My aunt stood next to me on the sidewalk looking at her burned-out house. I could see on her face that she could feel it too. That overwhelming pile-up of time gave her a blank, confused expression. She was standing on the sidewalk with me while somewhere she was watching her twenty-year-old son, Tanner, be carried out of the smoldering house in a black bag; and somewhere he was a baby, and she was teaching him to walk; and somewhere she was laughing with him in the kitchen as he made her breakfast. In the face of it, she had not only slipped between times, but she had decided to live in any time except this one. On that day, and for years after, she was utterly elsewhere.

We were there to retrieve some of my aunt's belongings, whatever had not been destroyed that she might still wear as she stumbled through the first few days. I followed her to the front door, and we each took a side of the plywood covering the entrance. It came away gently—almost welcoming, or maybe just pathetic. She walked into the house ahead of me because it was still her home and she had nothing left to be afraid of. To our right was a living room and the echoing dark of a cave. A vertical swath of grey sunlight came through the ceiling just above the kitchen where fire had eaten through the roof. A dusty tunnel of light, alive with moving particles like the deep ocean.

As we moved through the living room toward the hallway, I felt the kind of guilt one has when they fear touching the body of a newly dead loved one. It was the kind of guilt I would feel a week later standing over a coffin, terrified to touch the mass of flesh repurposed for mourning, ashamed that I could no longer recognize it as family.

Nothing had been touched since it happened. The coffee table, TV, couch, armchair, plants, coatrack, bookshelf, and every book on it was covered in a layer of ash. Any sense of home had been sucked out and replaced with the hollow sound of silence just after screaming stops. The walls must have been covered in blood, but I can't remember them that way. My mother remembers the bloody walls vividly, but somehow, they have been scrubbed from my memory. The details available to me are shrinking. Perhaps they had already been cleaned, but who would have cleaned them? They could have been taken for evidence somehow, but a wall? There are pieces and there are holes. Writing this now creates more holes; the memories become more unreliable when they are fixed with the wrong words, and they are always the wrong words.

My aunt's bedroom was at the end of the hallway. When we approached the open bedroom door, we saw that everything in the room was covered in the same grey layer of sediment, but underneath were little hills. Each dresser drawer had been emptied and its contents tossed about the room. It occurred to me for the first time that he had gone through her things. He spent *time* in her room.

As I write this, I can remember the sentence *he spent time in her room,* but I have trouble recalling the experience of seeing her room in disarray. Such is the benefit of finding words to weigh down the memory. Such is the cost.

But I remember the smell of smoke. Even when all detail is diligently washed away from memory, smell lingers. Nothing from the house on Elm Street would ever fully escape the smell of smoke. The various storage units my aunt used over the years to keep items salvaged from the house would all smell of stale campfire. The black-and-white-striped cardigan I wore into the house that day would be relentlessly saturated. I never could bring myself to wear it again. Neither could I bring myself to get rid of it.

THE NEED FOR A STORY is strong and in the stomach. In the aftermath, it pushes out most other needs. The pieces I have to build a story of the early hours of February 28, 2008 in the house on Elm Street are slim and incomplete but braid loosely together to create a nest for the story, if not the life of it.

The fire was reported by a passing stranger who noticed smoke coming from the windows around 4:30am. Firefighter Jason Atwood describes entering the home in his Observation Report:

> *Enter front door of the structure with my partner off the nozzle. Went into the kitchen where flames were visible. I then told FF Foster to put the fire out while I checked for possible victims. Upon finding the first vic I took off a glove and reached down to check and see what I had (wasn't sure what it was). That's when I realized I had a victim and couldn't believe what I saw but I did confirm an 1106.*

I enjoy the phrase *off the nozzle* as it is written in the report. I assume he means that he was not using oxygen, but I admit I have no knowledge of firefighting whatsoever, so it really could mean anything. I also like the frankness with which he writes. The step-by-step accounting of events. It's approachable and clear. Many of the court documents perch on the boundary between professional and decorative language about the murders. *"Trust no one", a broken heart, a knife, are symbols on a belt found in a plastic bag stuffed with the bloody clothes and a pair of bloodstained black Nike sneakers*...begins the prosecuting attorney's response to the first appeal, leaning unabashedly on the imagery.

My cousin is married to a Spokane police officer who heard about a fire at his mother-in-law's address over the radio and set off a chain reaction of phone calls through the immediate family. The woman who rented the basement bedroom of the house on Elm Street was asleep across town at her boyfriend's apartment as Tanner's blood seeped through the floorboards and covered the blue exercise ball next to her bed. Her cat was the only one living when firefighters arrived and found two dead bodies in the burning home. My aunt was also asleep across town at her boyfriend's home. Lucky chances. Lucky nights. She missed three panicked phone calls before she answered one.

As the news spreads and the sun begins to rise, a group gathers outside the still-smoking house. Tanner's cell phone will be called with increasing desperation. The restaurant next door will open early to let the family wait out of the cold. Officers will come to the restaurant to confirm there are two victims in the house, but identifications cannot yet be made. Tanner's cell phone will be called again as everyone refuses to abandon normalcy in the face of the impossible. The woman who rented the basement bedroom finally answers her phone and is taken off the list of possible victims. A police officer will come to the restaurant to ask my aunt if she has dental records for Tanner. No one will try his cell phone again. Everyone will gather in front of the home as the first body is brought out of the house in a black bag. My aunt will beg the officers to tell her if her son is in the bag. My mother will hold her sister from the waist both to keep her from charging the officers and from falling. My aunt will ask as though praying, *Does he have a tattoo of two music notes on his shoulder?* The officer will take pity and nod slightly. My aunt will slip through her sister's arms to the ground.

BY MIDDAY ON FEBRUARY 28, 2008, a young man named Justin Crenshaw was identified as a possible suspect in the double homicide, and the Affidavit of Probable Cause that immediately preceded his arrest was filed the next day. Justin's aunt told detectives that on the night of the twenty-ninth she was *reluctant to go home because she had a "knot in her gut" about Justin being involved in the incident on E. Elm.* The day after the murders, it was confirmed that the bloody fingerprint on the side door off the kitchen matched Justin. A month later, a stash of bloody clothing was found in his aunt's garage. The pile of evidence was absurdly complete. Justin only weakly attempted to hide what he had done, and as my family converged in Spokane, our suspense was short lived. We had a name and face by the end of the week. But we needed a story, so we started to build one.

Once, while living in Las Vegas, Justin Crenshaw attacked his friend for refusing to lend him his car. He stabbed his friend in the neck, tossed him a rag to stop the bleeding, told him to call an ambulance, and stole the car. Several people recounted this story to me in the weeks after the murders. This story was intended to illustrate his history of violence and his propensity for chilling emotional detachment. This story means: Justin is just one of those people.

The details may or may not be true. It is true that Justin spent eighteen months in a Las Vegas prison for attempted murder before he moved to Spokane. It is true that I was offered a perfect trajectory from his troubled past to a Las Vegas prison to my aunt's front door on Elm Street. I would like to reject this offer. I would like to understand but I'm certain I cannot, so I would like to ask questions.

I HAVE COME HERE TO DOCUMENT and to ask, can I move this way? As in decades?

WHEN MY MOTHER TOLD ME that her father had attended the last public hanging in Kentucky as a child, I remember thinking, *That's the kind of birthplace that doesn't let up.*

I don't know how he told the story to her, but she told it to me as evidence of something she needed me to understand; it was her birthplace too. What I understood was that my mother wanted badly for it not to be mine but, of course, it is.

What I didn't know when I first heard the story was that anyone who happened to live in or near Owensboro, Kentucky, in August of 1936 went to watch them hang a young Black man named Rainey Bethea, and a few thousand traveled from even farther. By most estimates, at least 20,000 people packed themselves tightly into the square, with some climbing lamp posts or onto the shoulders of a neighbor to get a better view. And somewhere in this sea of eager witnesses was the small round face of a tobacco sharecropper and his nine-year-old son, my grandfather Wilbur.

When I first heard the story, I pictured reluctance on the face of the small child. I pictured few other people there. I thought it was the kind of event that made a family like mine, that made a man like my grandfather. When I eventually saw the grainy photos of that day, the scene in my imagination broke down. Newspapers reported a spectacle and an audience with unmitigated exuberance. They reported it as undignified, which unsettled the country and helped push the machine of capital punishment out of public view. These reports were later corrected to say the enormous crowd was, in fact, nearly silent as the chaplain raised his hand. Thousands of hushed and merciless faces surrounded a man and waited for him to die. Thousands. My grandfather would have grown quiet. My grandfather would have watched.

Of course, this event was not an anomaly. This racist and cruel spectacle was utterly a part of everything that had come before it and everything that came after. It was the last public display of an institution, a machine that soon afterward moved indoors but never stopped churning.

I can't be sure, but I think my great-grandfather brought his son to an execution to learn a lesson about crime and punishment and white supremacy. I think he was poor and mean and wanted to feel powerful. I think he may have delighted in the death, although that is itself a cruel speculation. Watching a public murder, maybe my grandfather did learn a lesson. He learned about the system. He learned to watch and be entertained by its viciousness. He must have also learned something about dying.

There is a picture of Wilbur around the age he would have been when he watched Rainey Bethea die. It's a family picture that no one seems keen on taking. He is a blond child with overalls. He looks tired. It's hard to translate the face of this child into the looming presence he will become—but it's a short walk from the face of his father. Otho looks like he is angry because it's practical. Wilbur's mother Antha is thin and strong and unhappy because that is practical too. Wilbur's sister Clarissa squares out the image. She has a perfect blond bowl cut around her sullen face. All of them look like animals trapped so long they have stopped looking for a way out.

I wonder how chances are stored in the muscle. How many generations does it take before our cheekbones start to descend through our necks and settle in our chests? Antha's face seems as though it would be grey even if the photo was in color. None of them have any questions.

As a child, Wilbur waddled into the family barn to find his grandfather Counsil hanging from the rafters. This is a story about hanging. Counsil was forty-five years old and hanged himself from the rafters of the barn on the family's tobacco sharecrop in Kentucky. Wilbur was often just the right size to fit into the violent spaces of his father. These violent spaces grew more pronounced after the death of Counsil. Or maybe Wilbur got a little bigger and was able to fill them up more. Wilbur was a little boy when he found his grandfather's body, a few years before he was a little boy watching a whole city hang Rainey Bethea. This is a story about size.

There is a portrait of Counsil looking dead-straight ahead. It appears to be some kind of special occasion. His large but narrow frame takes up the entire image. He is clean-cut in a suit and tie. There is a large pin on each lapel and a handkerchief artfully puffed out of his jacket pocket. Somehow it is clear that this is a costume. His natural skin would more likely be denim, but it is difficult to tell if this is in the picture or in my blood. His head is strikingly rectangular, a rule that his hair and jaw follow. He looks like a charming vampire from a distant century. He looks thoughtful. He looks like my mother. He doesn't look suicidal. He looks suicidal.

Prosecutor Jack Driscoll filed for an extension the day before a decision was to be reached on whether he would seek the death penalty in the case against Justin Crenshaw. When asked by local news station KXLY, Tanner's brother said, *I'm not "oh forgive him." I have a lot of anger about it. If his life needs to be taken for what was taken from us, that's completely justified.* His comments were taken as basis for the news station to report that *members of Pehl's family hinted that they would support a decision to seek capital punishment.* There was no organized discussion among the extended family, and after many satellite conversations, no consensus. Immediate family spoke in private with Jack Driscoll, and when he decided not to seek the death penalty, no one seemed particularly angry. Driscoll was concerned about the difficulty of getting a conviction with the possibility of death looming over the jury and instead sought life without parole.

Comments from a now defunct website, www.topix.com/ JustinCrenshaw, steamed with the kind of visceral anger that is particularly terrifying when seen between strangers.

Stephanie Augusta, GA #138 Apr 5, 2009
Lethal injection is easy…he needs to hurt how they both hurt. I'd think Justin should stabbed and cut into pieces and burned like Sarah and Tanner. (sic)

passerby Renton, WA #143 Jun 28, 2009
HANG THE BEAST!

Justin would have been the first person sentenced to death in Washington State since 2002. There were eight men on death row when Washington State abolished the death penalty in 2018. If they had made it to the finish line, they would have been offered a choice between lethal injection and the state standard, hanging. Washington was the last state to have active gallows.

I recently rewatched *Dead Man Walking* because I wanted to put death at the distance, at least the distance between my couch and my TV. I wanted to remember how capital punishment looks through the filtered lens of an Oscar winner. The fictionalization of this story opens it up, helps it to be counted. Murder by the state is a strange, sloweddown way to look at death. So many deaths are not able to be caught or examined but here is death that doesn't *just happen*.

Susan Sarandon, with little makeup and big eyes, plays a hardkind woman better than anyone. We are intended to sympathize with her predicament and I do. She is trying to solve a puzzle that no one else seems to want solved. Everything is pink: pink houses, blouses, tablecloths, flowers. Pink is soft but complicated, not quite any one thing. *It's easy to kill a monster but it's hard to kill a human being,* says the lawyer. It's true and obvious. It's also demonstrably not true that proving yourself a human being will save you. The movie is trying to start from both the beginning and the end, to make sense of this system of brutal compromise after brutal act.

The whole topic makes me feel closer to religious than I am comfortable with. I'm tempted to resort to meaningless excuses like, *We don't have the right to take a life* or *who are we to play God.* It is more truthful to say that watching a skillfully controlled death perpetrated by an elaborate system we have created to bury the part of ourselves we are terrified to see makes me want to claw at time. I believe this machine says something grave about our tendencies. Out among all the death we cannot control—that I have not been able to control—this is death with an excess of time and audience. This is the performance of death. The performance of punishment. This is the convoluted core of humanity's systems that are intent on breaking and intent on blood. This is the system that my grandfather took as medicine.

The movie doesn't take a side. It shows the central death as a relief to everyone: the families of the victims, the nun, the ghosts of the dead, even Michael himself. His coerced confession gives him some catharsis which is then gifted to the audience to support us through the gruesome scenes of his preventable death. We are supposed to be comforted because at least we *know* he did it. When Michael (and the possibility of saving him) dies, so does the pink. Everything becomes a sweet, alive green: the house, the hallways, the buildings, even Helen's fucking blouse changes. Green seedlings of closure and reconciliation. A new hue to complete the circle as Michael is reborn into trees and leaves, now (and for the first time) a productive part of the earth.

I finish the film crying in rage. It's all just too complete.

ALMOST EVERYWHERE TESTED, THE BLOOD of the three was mixed together.

I have taken up pity.

THE ONLY PERSON EVER LEGALLY executed by Pacific County in Washington State was a man named Lum You. You was a Chinese immigrant and is overwhelmingly described by history as a charismatic and kind man. There were five hundred paper invitations distributed for the event, each with a name handwritten at the top and signed by the sheriff at the bottom.

You are respectfully invited to be present at the execution of
LUM YOU
Friday January 31, 1902 at the Pacific County Court House at
9:00 o'clock a.m.

Pacific County murders Lum You just a month before a law will require all state executions to take place at the state penitentiary in Walla Walla. In 1911, the small courthouse used to hang the well-loved man is boarded up and nearby a striking white building with a stained-glass dome is built. The new courthouse sits just across the valley from my mother's home. You can see it from her window. It's an obvious marker on the landscape, and even a quick drive down the 101 through town will expose its blatant elegance. There is nothing else like it in South Bend. It's a grand structure in a town with nothing grand. It sits on a small hill next to a Victorian pond with a little bridge that

I fed ducks from as a child. This is the beautiful building in which my grandfather Wilbur spent most of his short sentences for assault.

There is one other grand presence in South Bend: the deep green of the surrounding forest. Thick moss-covered evergreens protect the town on all sides and hold time in their branches in such a way that the hanging of Lum You in 1902 feels to me as present as any other event there. History stops meaning anything and means everything. The small patch of ground that once held the original courthouse is now empty except for the invulnerable maple trees. They call it Hangman's Park.

The circumstances of the murder You committed were understood by the community and almost no one believed he should be hanged for his crime. All the ways we are held by our procedure; all the ways we are drowned by it. Many petitions for clemency for Lum You were circulated but the churning could not be stopped. One petition was signed by one hundred women of South Bend. The *Seattle Star* newspaper reported at the time that *strange as the case may seem his strongest friends are the women of South Bend...* because, as the petition stated, *many extenuating circumstances should have been considered in the trial.* This is the machine: cruel, racist, and slick with momentum.

There is never enough space for the details. There was an unprovoked attack on You that preceded the murder. There was a plea to the sheriff by You for help. There was a miscommunication. There was a reluctant and pressured jury who expected a much lighter sentence. The women of South Bend do not seem an easy lot to sway to the side of an immigrant murderer in 1902. I suspect the errors were egregious. Almost everyone wanted to find a way out for Lum You. Reportedly, his jailors routinely left his cell door open hoping he would escape (which he did, but was soon after captured).

Lum You's last words are reported as being, *Goodbye, everybody, all my friends, women and men. Wish me all good luck...Kill me good.*

THE SECOND BODY IN THE house on Elm Street turned out to be eighteen-year-old Sarah Clark. Another branch with which to build the nest of a story. Sarah had a best friend and the best friend had a brother named Justin Crenshaw in Las Vegas whom she had never met. When Justin moved to Spokane, his sister embraced him in her life and introduced him to her best friend, Sarah.

In the winter of 2008, Tanner moved home to Spokane after a short stint in Olympia. He was twenty years old and took a job as a line cook at a restaurant just a short walk from his mother's house. Soon after Tanner was hired, Justin was hired as well. The time between their meeting and the murders is somewhat unremarkable. Justin introduced Tanner to Sarah. Tanner introduced Justin to his mother, sister, and roommate. The brief encounters that Justin had with the family would be played over and over in their minds, dissected to look for weaknesses in their ability to perceive what another person is capable of doing.

In a picture, Sarah leans back on a wicker chair in a blue floral dress and a backdrop of lively green. Her hair is dark and freshly cut. She is playfully bashful, but she is comfortable. She is unafraid.

The bodies of Sarah and Tanner reveal just a small pit at the center of the story, one which is delivered to the families shortly after the autopsies and never revised. Tanner's hands and forearms are covered in defensive wounds. He is stabbed in the head, neck, and chest repeatedly with a kitchen knife before falling in the hallway just off the kitchen. He has some blood in his lungs but most likely died as a result of blood loss after one blow severed an artery. Sarah is stabbed in the neck until her head is almost separated from her body. She is found sitting precariously upright with her head propped up by the bedside table. Both are covered by a blanket and stabbed through with the long decorative swords that had adorned the wall of the adjacent bedroom—the adolescent decorations of Tanner's brother. We know that the swords were put in place after both were already dead. We know the sword in Tanner lodged in his spine and when draped with a blanket gave the impression to the firefighter that he was uncovering a vacuum cleaner. On the official report, Sarah is simply noted as *in the east bedroom with obvious trauma to the body*. Sarah is found with a sword through her neck. Decorative.

It takes time for information to spread through the body. When I learn that Sarah was found with a fist full of her own hair in her hand, it takes time for me to know it. It takes weeks for it to come into focus and when it does I can't catch my breath. In a rush of panic, I describe to a stranger the scene I can't stop picturing—can't stop knowing— before running outside to vomit in the street. I sat for a long time on the dingy sidewalk, shaking and learning how to hold it; learning how to know that she had time to fight but only against herself.

I REMEMBER STANDING IN A garage around the time of Tanner's funeral. I remember standing in a circle with my cousins and my brother and a few of their friends when the topic first came up; Justin could be sentenced to death for this. I remember standing on the cold cement and seeing my exhales cloud and disappear. I remember feeling as though I did not speak the same language as the people around me, but that theirs was a language I had heard often as a child and which I could still faintly understand if I had a beer and a smoke and let my body relax into it.

When the death penalty came up, it hovered between us at eye level and then hit the ground in the center of the circle with a heavy thud that threatened to tip me over. My deeply held suspicion and revulsion at this practice came up through my chest and out of my mouth. *I don't believe in the death penalty. I can't believe in it now.* It was all one motion, but it was a new sensation, a new path, a new kind of death. The conviction now had to flow around Tanner's body buried in my stomach. I had to say that the man I know slaughtered Tanner in a hallway should not be killed for his crime. And not because it would be too easy. And not because it would be too expensive. And not because he may not have done it.

Justin Crenshaw moved about in the house with two dead bodies in the next room while still covered in their blood. He moved an oversize set of candlesticks from the mantel over the fireplace and put them in front of the couch in an unsettling arrangement that looked both illogical and willful. He took the family pictures from the walls of the living room and placed them face down on the couch cushions neatly in a row. Something he didn't want to see. Something he wanted to build. Something he wanted to unbuild. My aunt's living room was decorated in soft pastels with silver metal frames around stiff family portraits. Pictures with perfect smiling faces adorning a house that had all the warmth of mauve and floral and walking barefoot on fluffy clean carpet. It was the sort of living room that makes a half-hearted anti-altar like the one Justin left behind feel like an indictment of a whole way of life. Tanner's unfinished tax return was used as kindling to start the fire on the gas stove before leaving.

A few months before his death, Tanner learned to play "Disarm" by the Smashing Pumpkins on the guitar. In a video he made, there is no preamble, he just starts the song slow into the camera. He sits on the floor with his ratty jean-covered legs crossed and his back to a clean cream wall. His lisp makes the song feel tender and new. He repeats, *The killer in me is the killer in you.*

Justin has never admitted to remembering anything about the murders apart from the smell of smoke. It's the smell that sticks. But if the memory is actually gone, where did his culpability go? Did it disappear into the fire? Can blame evaporate? What do I do with his strange and deliberate actions after? What part of him came out in that impulse and where did it retreat to? If it retreated at all.

In his closing arguments, defense attorney Chris Bugbee asks, *Is he just somebody who, on the happiest day of his life, just decided in a very horrendous and gruesome fashion to kill two of the only people he could consider friends in Spokane, Washington? Or does it make sense that his brain was overcome with this condition?*

Bugbee argued at trial that Justin Crenshaw suffers from a rare disorder that makes him especially violent when he drinks and causes extreme memory loss. Bugbee's case takes only one day to put forward and includes only two witnesses on Justin's behalf. A friend recounts a story from their teenage years in which Justin acted erratically at a party. A psychiatrist testifies to the possibility of Justin having pathological intoxication or alcohol idiosyncratic intoxication and offers a number of stories as evidence, including the 2004 attempted murder charge in Las Vegas. Little research has been done on this condition, which is characterized by *aggression, impaired consciousness, prolonged sleep, transient hallucinations, illusions and delusions...followed by amnesia.* When asked if it is possible that Justin does not suffer from this particular disorder, the psychiatrist answered, *Yes.*

A request to test Justin for the condition is eventually denied by the judge. The test would have included Justin consuming a large quantity of alcohol while being observed by a specialist and there is no hospital in Washington or Oregon that would allow such a test at their facility. There is no attempt by Bugbee at trial to deny that Justin committed the murders or to account for his actions after. He relies heavily on our desire for answers. If his brain was *overcome,* then we have a story and we don't need to be afraid. *Does it make sense?*

I am just braiding the branches I can find. A branch: When the judge gave him the last of four opportunities to speak at his sentencing, Justin said, *No thank you, Your Honor. I don't want to take anything away from any of the families.*

If you search online for *Tanner Pehl and Sarah Clark murder,* you will find images of my family. As they speak to reporters, you will see that they are living a version of their lives they didn't know was possible. You can watch as it sinks in that this is the only version they will ever have. You will see it pulsing in their faces as they push their pain out into the camera hoping somehow to free themselves from it by making everyone understand that what has happened cannot happen. Most of the images and videos are taken in the parking lot of the neighboring restaurant. In one news clip, my cousin tells a reporter that her brother was loved but it comes out as though she is begging—and she is.

Your search will include an image taken from my Facebook page just hours after the names were released. The image is of Tanner on the back deck of my childhood home. He's wearing a baseball cap and posing for the camera. He was tired. He had just woken up. He was annoyed at my morning energy but decided to open to it. He always did. The image without context makes him look like trouble. When I see it in public, my whole body curls in at the edges. Another little death.

Justin Crenshaw wears a baby-blue jumpsuit. He wears a dark navy, well-fitting suit. He wears a denim blue short-sleeve shirt. He sits at the table with both hands folded under his chin. He sits at the table with one hand under his chin, resting his head. He is clean-shaven. He has short stubble. His hair is moussed up off his forehead. He has a goatee. He is rosy-cheek young. He is attractive. He is serious, hurt, and hollow. His face registers satisfaction just on the nice side of smug. He works hard to control and direct his effect. His body is straining to refuse anyone his contrition. He is shooting for neutral but missing. He looks exhausted and dark circles have formed under his eyes. He is battling hard not to remember, not to look as though he remembers. He shows something like sympathy but for someone far away, for a character in a tragic story he is being forced to listen to. He has a half-smile as he walks down the hallway of the courthouse. He enjoys being filmed.

LOOKING OUT FROM MY MOTHER's front window, I can imagine myself almost anywhere. I see a wall of lush green hillsides, and to the right, the town of South Bend appears and disappears around the curve of the river. This town has always made me feel as though I could stick to it like flypaper. I have difficulty seeing the place as just one of a type: small town, coastal town, logging town, ghost town. It has always been particular to and inextricable from my family, which is in turn inextricable from a rustic misogyny and the many wounds that won't heal in the damp. Sometimes I blame them for not being a family that knows how to hold onto the living.

My grandfather Wilbur was being followed around everywhere by the vaguely infectious shadow of a failed marriage when he met Bernice, the youngest daughter of a close-knit Catholic farming family just over the river in Indiana. Wilbur was funny. Bernice had narrowly survived a childhood battle with pneumonia, which left her with a long scar on her side and a deeply carved rebellious streak. Something about borrowed time—or at least I like to think so.

It was simple opportunity that brought Wilbur, Bernice, and their four children to live in Raymond, the small town nestled in close on the east side of South Bend. It was just a job out amid a green like they had never seen. After nearly sixty years in Washington, my grandmother Bernice still has a Midwestern sliding around of the words she uses to describe the wind or rain, but nothing surprises her. Everything *just is* and there is no use complaining about it. I can't remember a single time she has spoken longingly of another season or cursed the relentless chill. I enjoy thinking of her not yet thirty years old and in sparkling awe of a new place that has so much rain everything grows green all year round; an impossible green.

There is the story about a deer Wilbur poached one year. The deer Bernice hid in the dryer when the sheriff came by. The deer the sheriff found and fined them for having butchered. There is the story about the boys from town who stole all the meat in the freezer one year when food was already scarce. They smashed all the pies Bernice had made. It's a story with details I don't remember exactly but that makes my stomach sink when I think of it, the way I feel when I witness someone who is deeply embarrassed. This may be why I don't remember the details.

Sometime in the night, my mother wakes to the sound of her father coming home heavy. When the door opens, he is singing and swaying. He wakes up the girls who are pretending to sleep. *Do that song.* He will lift each feather girl onto the table and stumble back. *We have company. Sing that song I like.* The girls will stand on the kitchen table in their nightgowns and sing for their father's friends. My aunt will learn to pull nutrients from the attention. My mother will wet the bed that night.

My mother picks ferns for twenty-five cents a dozen all season to buy a catalog dress. Wilbur comes home swaying. My mother waits out the storm under the kitchen table, alone in the dark of the country. After Wilbur leaves the family to start another, Bernice becomes the first female employee at the shake mill. Bernice works the graveyard and her youngest, my mother, is often home alone. My mother wears the soft pink catalog dress to first grade. Wilbur shoots the family dog for the hassle. Wilbur drags his son into the woods to shoot the family dog. Layered time. Steady into steady dark. My mother hides in the cupboard at school; the soft pink catalog dress is see-through.

Why do I remember so keenly how to be embarrassed and where do I keep it so that it feels eternally ready to unholster? It has something to do with not enough food. It has something to do with my mother hiding and thinking she is wrong in the world. I know how to stand with my shoulders curled when I look at my pies all smashed on the ground.

My mother is asked to recount her heritage in class. She answers, *half-German, half-hillbilly* and is punished. Wilbur always had a way of making it sound not so bad to be what they were. The kind of birthplace that doesn't let up.

MY MOTHER AND I ATTENDED the visiting hours of Sarah Clark's memorial room while the ground was still iced over outside, giving the funeral home a slow, hibernation pulse. I had the overwhelming feeling that it shouldn't be open. We should close up death in the winter. Inside the small rectangle room was a miniature museum of Sarah's life. There was a collage of pictures and some personal items on display that reminded me of an exhibit on the sinking of the Titanic I saw once. The result was a flimsy replica of a life. Pictures of Sarah smiling bright and honest were the only items that felt acutely personal.

Sarah is not my family, but she has unwittingly become entangled with us. Her family is large, modest, and religious. On the wide spectrum of grief responses, the Clark family is on the opposite side from the Pehl family. Aside from sentencing, there were few images of them in the news. Their family turned inward to heal in what seemed like inverse proportion to mine.

The possibility that Justin was jealous of Tanner or rebuffed by Sarah is suggested lethargically at trial but not pursued. Those prone to commenting on online news articles love this version of the story. *Something in him must've SNAPPED. Total love triangle thing. He liked her, she probably was scared of him a little bit* (MyDeathSpace.com).

Jack Driscoll makes a counteroffer to Bugbee's medical acrobatics: Justin Crenshaw simply *has no conscience.* It's the sort of underdeveloped explanation that can only be found when the evidence is strong enough to drown out the need for reasons, when the only answer required is a simple yes or no to the question: Is Justin Crenshaw to blame? There was no attempt to understand Justin's behavior after the murders by either side. Driscoll said at trial, *It's not a whodunit…it's a trail of blood leading all the way to Justin Crenshaw,* and to Justin is exactly as far as any trail was followed. In the aftermath, the only thing vying for space beside the need for a story is the need for an ending.

SARAH AND TANNER ARE BOTH listed as victims in the 2008 Washington State Domestic Violence Fatality Review. Their names each appear just once, and the details of the case are not given. The report begins, *Between January 1, 2007, and June 30, 2008, 430 people were killed by domestic violence abusers in Washington State.* The report breaks down the deaths by relationship to the attacker and weapon used. It details the percentage of attacks that included children and how many of those children witnessed a murder.

Before I discovered their inclusion in this report, it had never occurred to me to categorize the murders of Sarah and Tanner as domestic violence. I am surprised by my willingness—almost eagerness—to not see these murders as part of a cultural pattern of domestic violence with such a fragile excuse as the short duration of the relationship between Sarah and Justin. *Read the report and remember the stories of those who have lost their lives to domestic violence* is the first recommendation in the section titled, HOW TO USE THIS REPORT AS A TOOL FOR IMPLEMENTING CHANGE. I wonder if Justin was violent with Sarah before the night of February 28. Reading the report, the story in my mind starts to widen at the edges to meet my understanding of domestic violence as it relates to larger social structures, i.e. strangers. Those edges also come up against the long history of violence in my family.

This is not my story, but if I do not form it into something I am afraid of what it will do to the air around me. I worry pieces of it will be inhaled by a child. I am afraid that what I form it into won't hold; that I cannot bind it and it will find its way into everyone not yet aware that it can never be buried.

ONE NIGHT WHEN BERNICE WAS sure Wilbur was going to come home swaying, she made a plan. She told the neighbors to call the police if they saw the house lights flicker and told the kids to flicker the lights when things went south. As instructed, when Wilbur's hands were tight around Bernice's neck and she started to turn that airless color of purple, my aunt ran to the kitchen lights and turned them on and off, desperately hoping the message would be received by the neighbors before it pulled Wilbur's attention from her mother's throat and toward her. My mother stayed under the kitchen table and let her older sister run across the room like a smaller, braver Paul Revere. Wilbur slept it off in the county jail for the next three months. My mother drew him pictures and Bernice took them down to the beautiful white courthouse. Violence braided around the evergreens like the heavy moss. My blood fiction.

What did Wilbur breathe into his body when he watched Rainey Bethea fall? Did I inherit it? Did his sister Clariss already know how to be embarrassed as she pulled tobacco worms from the leaves up and down the rows of the field? Did she already know there were things in her blood that would have to be fought back, drowned out?

I CANNOT ESCAPE THE DESIRE to write the letter that begins, *Dear Justin, you don't know me but...* and yet every time I start this letter, I wonder what it is that I am really asking, what is possible to learn and what he is capable of giving. The grand gesture of a reason is almost certainly not available. So, what would I say? Tell me what it means to dig into the grit of the earth and keep breaking the small bones of your hands on the shards of strength buried there before you were born. Are you sure of the power you send through the air? Were you sure then? Tell me about hunting.

All the threads of ourselves have been braided under our feet, the loudest voices of fear feverishly adding to the creeping ground so we can stand upright. These blistering moments when the threads come loose and tangle our ankles or catch the limbs of the person next to us and we cannot stop the whole system long enough to shout above it *This is not safety*, and when one falls into the twined mess we have built together, another falls on top of them and soon we are standing on bodies everywhere.

Justin has no answers because the question cannot be asked of him alone. One can be ingested by the machine, I promise. You have already been ingested by the machine. Look at your feet. You are already standing on bodies everywhere.

THERE WAS A SMALL WORN footpath that once led from Bernice's home across her field. The path ran parallel to the river and past the chicken coop and large apple tree that became heavy with green apples every year and ended at the old red barn that would be torn down in the mid-1990s. Once, we had a bonfire in the center of the field. My brother and my cousins and I played in the dark around the fire. I must have been five or six because the dark still held a special kind of fear and possibility. The memory is as though a dream. People and other nouns appear and disappear without explanation. Bernice suddenly by the fire with a package of raw bacon. I remember looking up at her. I remember her asking if we knew what would happen if we got too close to the fire; if we fell in. I don't remember answering. I remember the sound of the bacon hitting the fire. I remember the sight of the fat bubbling. This is what would happen to you. I remember learning that my skin could melt.

Later that night, while curled in a sleeping bag on my grandmother's floor in front of her sweet old wood stove, my childhood imagination built a little girl my age who could be separate from me. She had fallen into the fire and while burning crawled back toward the house. Her fat boiling and her skin crisping—the fire slowly consuming her legs and then her torso as she pulls herself along with her forearms trying to reach the house. Just before she makes it to the front porch, the fire wins and the rest of her body burns in the yard. I turned the story over and over in my mind. I could be this girl-bacon. I could be so ill-fated.

The next day and for the next years, walking that small worn path meant walking over the body and story of my mirror girl. She never made it home. The pies are smashed. The dress is see-through. We climb with our whole bodies and pull up the rope behind us.

WE ARE ATTACHED. Slipping—but attached.

Whether Justin Crenshaw has a conscience means nothing. It is a constellation that can be traced and retraced while there is still nothing but sky. His half-satisfied smile comes up against turning the family photos face down on the couch. His selective amnesia comes up against him asking Tanner if he was an organ donor two days before the murders. When Tanner said yes, Justin supposedly replied, *When I die, I'm taking all my shit with me.* When every corner of the story comes up against another corner, the weight drops into the fold. It cannot be enough that Justin Crenshaw has no conscience because it is not enough that Sarah and Tanner did have what Jack Driscoll would call a conscience.

There is no line with Justin Crenshaw on one side and my family on the other. The truth must be more like a body of water and we are all somewhere along the shore. The distance is punishing but if we walk long enough around the edge we find the far side.

Still, *long enough* might mean *as long as we have.* Time becomes relegated to the extremes: the stunted trudging of the aftermath on one end and the panicked frenzy of the attack on the other. Some great energies collided in the house and were trapped in the moment, altering everything in the space. The coffee table, TV, couch, armchair, plants, coat rack, bookshelf and every book on it became items left over. It is the reason watching crime scene videos feels like entering an ancient church. It is the reason an uninspired rambler on Elm Street became sacred.

And, there is the species of time reserved for murder by the state. Days that can be counted out. Measured into hours and minutes and meals. Finite time that becomes thicker as one is taken down the hall, until the words of the final command come out which will make time suddenly snap into nothingness.

There is the kind of time that Sarah must have experienced when she realized Justin was coming after her. There is the way time appears to me now, full of painfully sharp, accumulating moments and choices that would have been so simple to change but are in the past and out of reach. There is the time between when Tanner felt the first stab into his abdomen and the time he fell unconscious which is all the time there is.

It's not easy to say it *just happened* and leave it there drifting with nothing under it. Reasons are heavy and hold us together. There is a gravity of need pressing down on the edges of ourselves. And without reasons, *why* is just a useless morsel. Maybe the same can be said of a conscience. When it goes wrong, is it salty? I mean, for how long was it written and prepared? How many stars had to cross the sky at just the right moment so that all the sparks of consequence were ignited? And when you find yourself in the sites of all the time and memory of *just happened,* is there a way out?

On New Year's Eve 2006, my aunt threw a party in the house on Elm Street. It was a party that had effortless momentum. It was a party so warm I had to duck outside every hour or so to be revived by a cold breath of air and a chat with the smokers before diving back in through the side door off the kitchen. It was a glowing orange celebration that buzzed. All the stories we told were inexplicably funny, the games we played were bright with our enthusiasm, and near midnight, when my aunt brought her guitar from the hall closet, we took turns singing the family favorites as the drinks caught up to us. Tanner and I cheated together at the dice game and beamed together when we won.

Walking through the burned house, shoulder to shoulder with my aunt, I was trying hard not to touch my own experience. I looked across the room to the tunneling grey light streaming in through the ceiling of the kitchen and I could see myself two years younger sitting on the counter. I am swaying and singing "Bramble and the Rose" with Tanner who is standing next to me. It's a song our mothers have sung together our whole lives; it's a song we know like our own names. I am wearing a beige V-neck sweater and he has the proud, scruffy facial hair of an eighteen-year-old boy. We are drinking something alcoholic that tastes like sour candy and laughing. I can see myself there, oblivious of my future self across the room in the dark, covered in ash.

In a picture from the party, my brother, Solomon, is dancing with our mother in the house on Elm Street. The warmth itself is a third character in the scene. He has dipped her back almost to the floor where she meets the camera upside down. He is smiling wide and open. They both have red, tipsy faces. It's a brand-new year.

mercy

Mercy: That which arrives in time and exceeds the reasonable.

—AB Huber

On January 3, 1992, my father wrote the following in his journal:

Was thinking about death last night. Pleasantly, mind you, about how I wish to be disposed of. I've said cremation and scattering my ash remnants on Davis Peak by the cabin. No change there but I hate to lay the burden on someone to accomplish this task that wouldn't enjoy the ascent to that beautiful mountain. If anyone is out there reading this and looking for information on unburdening themselves of my final compressed version and are not keen on the idea of a 5-mile hike to do it, just fertilize a nice big tree with me. I feel that I owe the earth my body in a condition that is easy to recycle.

Some years before he wrote those words, some years before my brother and I were born, my father will take a solo camping trip to the Quinault Rainforest—a wild and healthy green muscle on the Olympic Peninsula. He will carefully position his camera on the open tailgate of his Toyota pickup truck and walk briskly across the forest floor as the timer clicks. The camera will capture the image of a man in his early twenties in a rust-red sweatshirt and light blue jeans leaning against the base of an imposing cedar tree and the yellow tail of his dog blurring the corner.

After my father takes his own picture with the cedar tree, he will camp that night with his pickup truck and his dog. In the night, he will have a seizure.

Many years and many seizures later, the atmosphere is lost. My father struggles to breathe. He tells me there is a picture of a tree. I look through a stack of family photo albums to find it. When I bring it to him, he nods and says, *Yes, this one.* This will be the tree.

In 1958, my grandmother Alice wakes to a late-night phone call. Her husband has been in a car accident. She rushes to dress and wake her young son, my uncle. When she arrives, there will be no one there to help. There are gaping holes in this story. I am led to believe no one wants to help my grandfather out of the car. I am led to believe there may be a reason they do not want to help him. Alice wrestles her husband from the car and only the next morning at the hospital will she realize that she has severely injured her back. She will be instructed to spend the rest of her pregnancy indoors and in bed.

Over half a century later, my uncle will speculate one afternoon while having lunch with me that a lack of Vitamin D in utero could have triggered his brother's multiple sclerosis. He finishes his Diet Coke and muses, *What if Mom had been able to go outside?*

THE DETAILS AVAILABLE TO ME are shrinking. Was it my grandfather in the car accident or another man? My mother says that it was she who found the picture of the cedar tree for my father. The memory of finding the picture myself starts to become fuzzy. There is nothing around it. The instability of grief-time.

I drive up the winding road from Bernice's home to the cemetery and can't remember in which section I will find Tanner. I park and walk the aisles. He is much closer to the bottom of the hill than I remember. I recognize the names of those buried around him but cannot recall their relationship to one another or to me. Memory like a slick oil painting that never dries. Every time I bump into it I smear a little more around the edges. The trees make a sharp whistle. At least, I think it's the trees. Suddenly, it could be any number of things.

In the VA hospital in Seattle, my father is trying to sleep but a large florescent light has been left on over his bed. He can neither walk to the other side of the room to turn off the light, nor would he be able to reach his hand up to flip the switch if he could get there. He lies under the light, which both pulls him up like an alien abduction and pushes him down into the thin mattress with its incessant vibrating beam. He tries to shout through the door to the shadows of the night staff as they walk down the hall, but his tracheotomy makes it impossible. Maybe if he could reach his hand to his throat to close the airway long enough to make pressure enough to force his vocal cords into submission, but he cannot lift his hand that far. His throat and the door and the light switch may as well be a galaxy—the vastness and all.

Finally, a young man notices my father. Either he somehow hears the gasping, or he happens to look into the room and see my father straining his face and motioning with his eyes. The young man tries but he cannot understand the whistling emanating from my father's neck. He finds a pencil and paper and holds my father's hand and helps him form five letters: LIGHT. The man looks confused and sounds out the word, *lye-get? What is a lye-get?* My father sucks in a deep breath through the tube in his neck.

What do we do when the space in the room is a galaxy of light and we want to die in the dark? When all sense of self has been buried before your death and the only one listening outside your own head appears to share no language with you? Our harshest light.

My father summons his strength to try a phonetic translation: LITE. The man turns off the lights.

WHEN MY FATHER LAY UNCONSCIOUS, threaded with a tube for feeding and a tube for breathing, the doctor said they could remove the feeding tube, but they could not help him die. They would starve him to death, but they would not help him.

In 1990, my father began a journal covered in a soft blue cloth with flowers and polka dots. My mother bought it for him for Christmas and he wrote in it dutifully. The first entry is on Christmas day. The big news is that the stove is broken, it's snowing, and my brother and I have started to share a room. I am almost three years old. Presumably this means Solomon was just big enough to sleep in a bed and not a crib. The house sounds cheerful.

On January 2, 1991, he begins his entry this way:

> *Thought I may take a minute to state my position on an issue recently in the news. Parents of a girl, somewhere back east, tried to end her life support after she spent 9 (nine) years in a vegetative state due to an auto accident. Lawyers said the parents needed to prove that she would have wanted to die. Well, I'm now stating that I wish to die if I have irreversible brain damage. There, I said it!*

When he wrote this, he was the same age as I am now. It felt far away to him then. A thought experiment. A news story. As Jack Kevorkian became famous, shouting at the world from the cover of magazines, my father was still able to walk. Did he discuss Dr. Death? He already had the diagnosis. He knew that patients of Kevorkian had MS. He had to know.

What a gift to choose the day. Not to wait until the decay takes over, until you can no longer speak or beg or run from what chases you. Not to die in the crisp bright sick of the hospital, but to contemplate. To take control.

Still, how difficult to say *this* day and not that day over there. The pain it takes to be so certain.

My FATHER WAS DIAGNOSED WITH multiple sclerosis at the age of twenty-one. At the time, it didn't occur to anyone that it would kill him. He managed the symptoms as they came. By thirty-two he was married with two small children. As he slowed, as he was overtaken, he was caught wanting to know what his children would look like the next day. How we would grow. I often feel guilty for not having told him to go. Not letting him leave when he was suffering.

Medically assisted suicide is the opposite of murder by the state in every way. Time to decide. Time to make clear. Time to examine. Time to look to what comes next after time to ask questions. As I write this, there are twenty-eight states in which one can be sentenced to death against their will. There are five states that allow one the right to die with dignity.

I remember my father sitting up in his medical bed, pulling the elastic bands tied to the metal sides with handles and trying to exercise his dying muscles. He strained to laugh. He watched his kids come and go. He saw people walk across the room as he had once done so easily. He said, *I am done*, but he had no recourse to make it so.

I wish I could have made it nicer. I enjoy seeing death as not only inevitable but precious—something that can relieve and soften, a gift.

It's a wolf moon today. A glow of fire surrounds, but I resist any efforts to cleanse me of my dead. When I try to write down the details, I must confront the fact that I don't know a lot about my father, nor the disease that destroyed him.

Multiple Sclerosis: The History of a Disease is a 580-page book published just a year after my father's death. Somehow, I find it offensive to imagine MS didn't come into existence just to invade my father. Still, there is family lore about a great uncle who died of a mysterious slowing down. It's a phantom. It's a general weakening that eventually crushes.

I knew my father as an actor in the role of father—and he was utterly convincing. He made us believe with him in the next treatment or therapy or activity he could still do that would make his life fulfilling. He was so convincing that I could not see his pain as having a body. I could not recognize it as the pain I would feel if my body started to slowly rot beneath my brain, each day able to do just a little bit less. He knew he was going to die, and he fought without mercy for himself to keep his mind and decaying body in the world for us as long as he could, to teach us what he could, to comfort us when he could.

BEHIND HIS CRAFTED SHELL WAS a man trapped in an agonizing countdown. A terrified man. A heartbroken man. My mother remembers him in the cracked moments crying in frustration that he could not dress himself or comb his hair the way he wanted. He always did appear to me slightly disheveled, but I had no other image of him which I could compare to the wrinkled sweatpants or the flakes of dried white that clung to the corners of his eyes, which he could not lift his hand to his face to rub away. No image apart from the one cultivated by the inexperienced but affordable caregivers who came in and out of his life. It is my mother who remembers him choking on tears as he said, *I just miss hugging people.* My mother did her best to wrap his atrophied arms around her. An open love.

I know he was competitive. He liked to win at board games, especially trivia, and he was exceptionally good at them. I know he was frugal—a trait which allowed him to purchase his childhood home from his parents at the now unthinkable age of twenty-six and make it my childhood home. I know he liked comics, both drawing and reading them, as well as crossword puzzles, dad rock, and weed. I know he was funny, generally optimistic, and very excited to be a father. I know he was pescatarian and that he liked a veggie sub with everything on it except black olives. But this is a list, not a person. Knowing a person takes time, and time I didn't get.

A WARM ROOM STILL MAKES me claustrophobic. My skin closes in around me. Hot air feels insufficiently oxygenated. I panic. The feeling of sweat dripping down my spine, sucking my shirt tight to the skin and then pooling at the base of my back, elicits in me an almost instant rage.

If you have multiple sclerosis, chances are very good that heat can render your muscles putty in a matter of minutes. The anxiety produced in me by heat might be a reaction to my grandmother Bernice trying to sleep in the sticky-hot Indiana summer, or the reserve of excess flesh I have had on my body since college and which I often joke keeps me insulated from the cold but which also layers me like a heavy coat, or my great-uncle training in the sweltering heat of North Africa in 1943. But at its core, I suspect it comes from watching a man be repeatedly melted into a lump of useless flesh.

There was a mid-stage point in my father's illness that coincided with my fifth-grade soccer team playing in a local tournament. My father was an active supporter of my short-lived soccer career and drove me and my brother to the event in his modified minivan. With the push of a button, the side door would slide open, the entire vehicle would lower, and a ramp would extend from the floorboard to the ground. After the game and a few hours in the sun, we were ready to go home. I pushed the button and my dad drove his motorized wheelchair into the van. But at this point a small feat of Olympic strength was required. He had to hoist himself up with his arms and shift his body from the wheelchair to the driver's seat.

The afternoon had been especially warm for Washington. He strained to lift his body but collapsed between the seat and wheelchair, with his leg painfully contorted under him. He recognized his situation immediately and told me to find help. I ran from the van and looked for help. What does help look like? It didn't look like my ponytail and shin guards. The tournament had included dozens of teams and no one around me was familiar. Is help a stranger? Help had better be a strong stranger. Help had to be a stranger who would follow me back to a van, to the crumpled, vulnerable pretzel that was my father and straighten him out.

I found a man with a face I don't remember. The neighborly man asked another man to join and together they lifted my father into his seat. My father thanked them. He turned the car on and sat in the air conditioning until his muscles regained their shape. I knew he had no choice but to ask, but I felt as though my body were a glowing neon sign for sickness, spectacle, and sadness that shone across every field. I was the spectacle of him. I know where embarrassment lives in my body. I wanted to say to the man that my father will be strong when he gets cool again. I wanted to say he is very funny and very loved—to make excuses for the death at my door.

Six months later, my father's foot will get caught under the brake pedal while driving down a four-lane highway. Unable to stop, he will careen over the median and into the wall of a department store. It will make the local news. My father will make jokes about stunning the bystanders by pressing the button and driving out of the van like from a spaceship. His friends will laugh because he is funny. Later they will worry. He won't drive again.

My father is dying in the home on the field. His spine is showing through his skin. Scans of his brain show a large gray mass of raincloud over the delicate. The doctors say, *progressing* and *hallucinations*. I say, *Trust me. There are no snakes.* Storm clouds gather over the delicate. He says, *They seem so real. There are snakes everywhere.* I ask him my name; a beginning to come back for. He says my full name slowly—the way one can only do if they have named you, as though it was the only language he was sure of—and I am relieved he knows it. *I wouldn't lie to you. There are no snakes.*

When my father finally died, it was less *succumbed to* than *ingested by*. I had just turned seventeen.

THE MERCY IS TO BE ALIVE in the aftermath, to put the body in a box.
It's a furious unmaking, this process of being buried.

AFTER MY FATHER DIES, I imagine him in the context of a beyond and it occurs to me that if there is an afterlife, he won't be trapped in the decaying body I've known. Suddenly, a loss more absolute than his death. I mourn a man already a ghost of himself, a man who died slowly through tracheotomies, bed sores, feeding tubes, and hallucinations. A vacuum of the light into chaos. I want reunion with the ghost and the ghost is the one person I am sure cannot exist.

A calming water comes to cool the frenzy of the tide: if an afterlife exists, it must have a new set of rules, and what purpose can it serve to apply our rules to a game that requires death before entry?

THE DECK FOR THE HOUSE on the field is bulky and stable. It will splinter over the years despite the coats of deep red stain. The nails will work themselves back out of the wood slowly and without consensus. I have always known there are places burning into the center. It is green and full here. Plant the tree that will remember. *It is gravenstein season, your mother's favorite.* All along the rockery is the time it will take. I can touch the hen and chicks, lilac, and hydrangea. I can smell the cut grass. We cannot even understand our spring. Slowly it is made remembered, unburied and opened.

It will always remind me of your mother, my father says, holding the space between my cells in the front pocket of his button-up shirt as he builds me something to live in.

This is a dream and not a story. My father sits at the center of a room and a doctor says, *We're putting him down.* Sterile. Distant. I wake shaking and pull my knees up to my chest to know this is not the way it will happen.

When it happens, it will feel more like letting him down slowly from a cliff he is falling from anyway, his body heavy at the end of our ropes designed to keep him steady. It will feel like he is being pulled gently by the tide down below—like his hand left holding mine as he falls toward some beach of his own in the fog.

A kindness. An unkindness. It will feel like driving home through saltwater.

ON MAY 10, 1994, MY father wrote in his journal:

> *My Betaseron (Beta Interferon 1B) lottery number came up.*
> *Hopefully, this "miracle" drug will do what Imuran has not. The*
> *cost is more than someone without insurance could bear, I mean*
> *if you can't afford coverage you certainly can't pay 1000.00 per*
> *month for a drug. Will it stave off the M.S.? I sure hope so.*

My father writes this the same year that Oregon became the first
state in the US to legalize assisted death.

There were 67,000 people entered into a lottery for the new MS
treatment Betaseron in 1994. My father's number comes up in May.
It's an experiment. He is hopeful. The last entry in the journal is made
June 6, 1994—a full ten years before he dies but the date marks a shift
from mostly healthy and hopeful toward increasingly irritable, unstable
on his feet, dizzy, tired, numb, confused, divorced, dead.

Once when my father was rushed to the hospital, his dentures were left behind in a cup next to his bathroom sink. Without them, his cheeks were concave and his face looked strange, hollow, alien. He never let anyone see him without his teeth. Somehow in the rush of the paramedics and ambulance, his glasses were misplaced as well. He woke, hours later, in a hospital room without teeth and surrounded by a blurry room. He could not move his body. He did not understand where he was. A nurse told him that he was in the VA hospital in Seattle. He had stopped breathing in the night and was breathing through a hole in his neck now. All the while his skin sagged from just under his cheekbones toward his chin without scaffolding. He was forty-three years old. Someone eventually located his glasses in the back pocket of his motorized wheelchair. My uncle drove to his brother's home and pick up his dentures. My father slowly came back into a vaguely familiar shape.

These are the moments I wish I could take away from my father and replace with a celebration of his humor and compassion and a chalky drink he slurps down in sixty to ninety seconds. I wish I had been older. Old enough to hold his hand without trying to hold him in the world.

WE ARE STANDING IN A FIELD—twisted peaceful like a filbert.

My father intended to die at home. He signed a DNR and went back to his house to wither as long as it took, but when he stopped breathing again, his caregiver panicked and against instructions called the paramedics. He was intubated and transported to the hospital to die. He never regained consciousness.

We had already become accustomed to the wilted salads in the cafeteria; to the special room they offer families when their loved one is on the brink. I am trying and failing to eat a piece of browning iceberg lettuce drenched in ranch dressing when a nurse comes down the stairs and says, *He took his last breath a few minutes ago. You may want to come say goodbye.*

Was he still dying as I held his hand or was I minutes too late? His mouth was a little open. His mother, Alice, kept saying, *He's running now, he's running now.* I didn't think he was running. I wanted to pull him back into his cruel body and make him stay there. We walked out of the room and silently took the elevator to the parking garage. We divided into our separate cars and drove home. We left him there on a narrow hospital bed with his mouth open.

MOUNT ST. HELENS ERUPTS. MY mother is leaving work to find her car covered in ash. My father is building a deck for the house on the field and looks up at the grey. Something is coming. The ash starts to fall. The mercy is the scattering. The mercy cannot be the scattering.

In 1986 my mother and father are married and build a family in the home on the field. My mother learns the words *Grand Mal* and *Dilantin*.

We know the rock is filthy and still we rest our head. We haven't been able to unlearn so we climb with our whole bodies and pull up the rope behind us. We begin with our faces at the chain link. Wading into the slanting field as it tips slowly, as the whole of it becomes unleveled before me, as our feet dangle from the edge of the garage whose stone and wood we know like before death.

In the home on the field, my parents will have two children. My mother will try to invent a new history for them. Burn down the broken, the forest, the muddy shoes, but the stories will persist. Blood can't be retrained.

My brother Solomon comes out hard. My mother will name him after the anesthesiologist because Dr. Solomon will feel like God when he relieves her pain. I decide that the round little boy is mine the moment I see him. I am not quite two years old, but I know this child. I resolve to teach him everything I have learned in my short time in the world.

We will be in this together.

inheritance

I'm afraid that not even God understands that human sainthood is more dangerous than divine sainthood, that the sainthood of the laity is more painful.

—Clarice Lispector, *The Passion According to G.H*

IN 2012, MY AUNT CALLED me at work and said, *Solomon is missing*. He had been missing for three days. He left his house at 3 a.m. with a friend and didn't return. He left his dog at home and had no plans to be away.

The rest of that day is the memory of my skin on fire and trying to get out of it. A friend picked me up from work and drove me home. And as we drove, we speculated. He must have gotten into some kind of trouble. We should be calling hospitals, police stations, friends. He could have relapsed. But even as the possibilities came out of my mouth, my mind refuted each. He could call from a hospital or police station. He would never leave his dog, not even during a relapse. Something was very wrong.

My mother was coordinating people trying to help. I would get a few moments on the phone with her before being passed to someone else. My friend was trying to book me a flight from my home in California. I gave her my credit card but couldn't help her make any plans. The mountain roads between his home and town needed to be searched. There were hillsides to examine. There were back roads to scour. My mother called me from the side of a ravine, out of breath, searching. She said, *You need to get someone with you*. She didn't want me alone when I got the news she felt certain was coming.

In panicked time, my brother's body is sent spinning. The car lands upside down in a small area of city runoff water on the side of the road.

His body remains in the passenger seat, next to the dead body of his friend, suspended in the muddy cocoon of the old convertible he had purchased just a month before. The soft top of the car matches the spongey texture of the mud and together they conspire to become a sprung trap for the two. Both my brother and his friend drown.

There are infinite questions. How long did they try to free themselves? How long did they struggle? Did my brother have time to make an effort to reach for his pocketknife or did he just pull at his seatbelt with his hands? Could one have seen the disturbance on the surface of the water as they wrestled under it? When exactly, which second, did the water become still around the four tires peeking out from the surface? Was the radio on? If so, would I have been able to hear it from the road, still playing underwater?

Time in the following days had dull edges. Time slowed, changed, echoed. Solomon became *the body*, and the body became a part of the water for three days before they were found. On the forearm of the softening body was a large black tattoo of two music notes bracketed by the words: *Tanner Pehl* and *Never Forget*. Solomon was twenty-three years old. We were supposed to be in this together.

Now, I am on this beach learning to swim once again in the flat shadow of what is left, and you, Solomon, have become all beings with eyes.

I ARTICULATE MYSELF in their wake.

WE ALWAYS CALLED BERNICE'S SPARE room the *red room* because of a
long rectangular florescent light built into the transom above the door,
which was covered in a textured crimson plastic that made the room
glow red. I'm not sure when it was installed or if there is any decade
in which it would have been fashionable. The red room was one of
only two small rooms in the house. I remember it as cold and a little
dusty. White lace curtains draped over the window that looked out at
a road that was just miles of gravel when Bernice moved to Raymond.
As children, Solomon and I would join our cousins in games of gentle
magic under the red glow. Light as a feather, stiff as a board.

In the closet of the red room was a floral shoebox of notes, letters,
newspaper clippings, and other ephemera of Bernice's life. Once when
I was a teenager, I sat with her on the bed as she rifled through the box
for the evidence she needed. She pulled out a small piece of folded
paper and a rusted Purple Heart. She said, *Anything to know.*

That day I inherited a claim without details.

Now, I dig at the crumbling pieces of the story because the language
of the dead is seeping in through all my open windows. My father is
dead. My cousin is dead. My brother is dead. I wake with it. I stray.
I hold the same thin piece of paper that Bernice held in 1943 and I
feel her twelve-year-old hands. I feel the crowding of the time between
the day the letter was delivered to the farmhouse in Indiana and the

strangled moment in which I fall to the floor in my bedroom when I learn that my brother is dead. I wonder if my grandmother fell when she learned her brother had been killed.

When I was eleven, I fell in the gravel driveway as my sick dog was taken away to be put down. When did I learn to fall? I remember falling. I don't remember being taught.

On Solomon, I can never find the words. Like writing an essay on my left arm after it has been torn off. It's just searing. It's just blinding. The death of the sibling is the death of the self and one cannot eulogize oneself because the words are always outside of the body. When Solomon died, my life divided, narrowed in experience from shared to solo, and no flower nor song nor sunset could shield it.

But, I reasoned wearily and wounded, if I could not find Solomon alive, maybe I could find someone else who was sucked out of the world without explanation. Maybe I could find my great-uncle in death. *Anything to know.* Maybe I could give him back to my grandmother. Maybe it would make her whole. And, maybe, making her whole would make me whole.

WHAT DOES IT MEAN to be missing?

It means you are a saint. Only saints can be missing.

I AM UNPREPARED FOR MILES. I have a letter, a Purple Heart, and a name. I scratch out a painfully incomplete timeline:

November 15, 1942: Fritz turns eighteen
March 18, 1943: Term of enlistment begins
November 29, 1943: Fritz Relleke KIA

I send a letter to the government requesting the details via the Freedom of Information Act (FOIA). I agree to pay research fees as advised by online forums. The field is burning. There are records and the fire of records. *It may take up to 48 weeks to receive a scanned copy of the Individual Deceased Personnel File (IDPF).* Fees have been waived due to familial connection. It seems I have inherited something. According to the internet, Great-Uncle Fritz would have gone first to North Africa for training.

Bernice says, *They needed replacements, that was what he was.* I watch video of the Allies marching into Naples. Stop. I stray. I dig gracelessly into the need for it.

Bernice remembers hearing "Till We Meet Again" on the player piano at the farewell party. She softly sings me the chorus. She says, *He just cried and cried when they told him.* I think of Solomon at eighteen years old pretending to be big.

Where is it saved in the body when Fritz cries with fear, his round face heaving? His sister holds it in her stomach as he smokes a cigarette and reports for war. I know this because I have seen Bernice hold many things there. It's where I keep it all too. *Every tear will be a memory, so wait and pray each night for me, till we meet again.* I stray.

THERE IS NO DISTINCTION in the records between *enlisted* and *drafted*.

BERNICE DOESN'T RECALL THINKING ABOUT the wars she has lived through since the one that took her brother. She seems surprised by the idea of them. Her two boys were just barely too young for Vietnam. Otherwise, world politics was just a story happening in the background. It's too big to see unless you're right on top of it.

Bernice gives me a typewritten history of her mother's family. Compiled in 1990, the empty dashes after the births of those still living keep them living. My own dash, next to the dash of my father, next to the dash of my brother, just a few lines from the dash of my cousin. I pen in three new dates of death. There is nothing mentioned about our drinking gene. Our weaponized humor. Our affinity for music. Our violent tendencies.

THERE IS SOMETHING CHEMICAL THAT changes in the instant of suffering. I know it somehow in the way I know plants grow toward the sun, make choices. In a book about generational trauma, the author explains a situation with a client in which they experience a strange cold sensation and insomnia. The author diagnoses the client with leftover trauma from an uncle who froze to death at a young age. I put the book down. This is not the generational holding I was looking for.

The idea that we carry trauma in our cells and pass it along—that we remember in our bodies the way our ancestors shivered—makes sense to me. The idea that we are connected in ways we cannot always articulate feels deeply true, but I find when this author tries to tie his client to an uncle with a perfect line I want to scream. I want the author to say this is more complex than we will ever know so we must feel our way through it.

At the same time, I know there is something chemical that changes in the instant of suffering.

It's the moment in science fiction in which time is reset and horrific events have suddenly not happened. We are supposed to be comforted by the characters starting over and the pain having been erased. Truly erased. But I have always had the impression, the suspicion, that it could not possibly work this way. Even if, in some mystical world, the events have been overwritten with a happy ending, the *happening* of them in the world couldn't be. Suffering embeds itself in the crevices of time and does not let go. This common dream seems to be a nod to our deep desire to say, *Time eventually scratches out pain.* And while I understand the want, I think as we experience time as being of the present, all around is still the screaming of suffering in the past and future.

Term of Enlistment: *Enlistment for the duration of the War or other emergency, plus six months, subject to the discretion of the President or otherwise according to law.*

I highlight references to the 36th division—a calculation based on the few dates I have and some rough estimates. Fritz would have left New York for North Africa in the summer or early fall of 1943. I wonder if I have correctly identified the 36th division. There are many and they move and change. Excavation. *He just cried and cried.* No, the dates are wrong. Fritz was in the 45th division which moves in tandem with the 36th through the landing at Salerno. Bernice doesn't remember hearing about Salerno. The landing takes longer than expected. On the boat they stew their uniforms in coffee, afraid the original beige color will be too light for the mud, too available. This is a test. Fritz is waiting offshore for at least three days. The shore is bright with neon colors to mark landing points. Concertina wire. I wake desperate. *Anything to know.*

WE STAND HERE BRACED AGAINST IT. A system of occasions. The Relleke family makes a request for an exception: the last working boy on the farm. The request is denied.

Bernice says, *They all wanted letters.* She writes to a friend of her brother's named Alex Quintana. She writes Alex Quintana letters until he sends a letter that starts *Dearest darling* and twelve-year-old Bernice tells her mother. In 1994, Bernice gets a computer and tries to search for Alex Quintana. Soon after she gets rid of the computer for the trouble but trails like these can become wider when farther away. I find him easily. Alex Quintana survives the war and marries shortly after. He dies in New Mexico in 1990.

I highlight all references to the 45th.

I wonder how I learned to fall to my knees in the face of death.

A YELLOWED TACTICAL BOOK LAYS out the movements like a recipe. *After 19 November, 1943 the 45th held hard won positions among the eastern slopes of Sammucro and high ground above Venafro.* Hard won. If Fritz has lingered, where has he lingered? He can surely see Venafro. *Their mission was to open a portion of the Filignano-Sant-Elia road.* I layer a map of these abstractions onto a map of roads now in use. The Allies land at Salerno, the beach changes hands four times in as many days. Held down. They move slowly north.

These are the lines and the complications: The 45th comes up against the Gustav Line and then the Winter Line. The line cuts Italy in half across the middle and keeps them for winter. Fritz would have learned the words for *bleeding* and *medical attention* in Italian. *At 0600 on 29 November, 1943, the 1st Battalion 179th Infantry began the attack on the right flank but met small-arms, mortar and artillery fire.*

THERE IS A SINGLE SURVIVING picture of Fritz in uniform. A moment during his five-day furlough in the summer of 1943. He is round in front of his home in Indiana—unbuttoned and smoking, cocked hat, high-waisted pants. He is becoming buried. A clothesline defines a fierce break a quarter into the picture, just above his head. He is not at attention, he is mimicking attention. A sense of the ridiculousness in the certainty. A composed image, a mothering. A bit of Solomon maybe in the cheekbones, maybe in the refusal. On either side of the moment, a saunter, a cigarette, a five-day furlough.

One cannot be alive to see this. The same image as seen from standing with my ankles in the water, my back to the farmhouse. Six thousand Purple Hearts are brought to Salerno. There are not enough.

THE MAN IN THE DOCUMENTARY says, *Seasickness and fear make for an interesting combination. They vie for dominance.* Replacement depot. Heavy winter. Until no longer needed.

A folded yellow letter from Fritz to Bernice in a floral box:

> *You said that you hope I never have to but if I ever do I should kick the hell out of him or shoot his gizzard out. I didn't shoot his gizzard out but I shot his brains out and believe it or not he had a few brains.*

The chemical suffering of some other family. Nearly everyone who lived in Haubstadt, Indiana, in 1943 was a first- or second-generation German immigrant. Points on the field.

A point: *half-German, half hillbilly.*

BERNICE SAYS, *We got a letter starts: greetings.*
Bernice says, *It's an old joke but true.*
The letter starts *greetings* before it pulls you to your knees.

In 2020, Bernice needs surgery. She is in congestive heart failure. She is entirely blind. She cannot see the nurses and doctors who come and go from her room without a word. She wakes in the blur to footsteps and thinks she has lost her hold on reality, but she hasn't. She is awake in another time. The surgeon promises to take excellent care in her surgery, promises that Bernice will survive. She says, *Please don't do too good a job* and means it. She fears burdening her family. She fears slipping away slowly. She survives the procedure and is a little disappointed to wake up.

Bernice would like a way out. She is done. She'd like to stop the machine. She would like to be let go. Bernice and I share being thirty-three years old in 1962 and 2020 respectively. Time is a trap. Bernice wakes in the middle of the night grasping at the plastic mask over her nose and mouth. Then she remembers that she needs the mask to breathe now. Fritz has been dead for seventy-seven years.

I DON'T KNOW HOW TO make a home among the wild and tedium of grief, in the memorial stomach. But I identify passionately as a body in mourning. A consequence. A product. I once heard CA Conrad say, *Reincarnation is just struggling all over again.* It suddenly strikes me as odd that reincarnation has ever been comforting to anyone.

Bernice reads a poem of mine and says, *I like the way you brought Sol's thing into it.* She says, *I don't want to say "death"*—but she does. In a lavender evening of our history I wonder, are we sure we are constant?

Judith Butler writes, *Freud reminded us that when we lose someone, we do not always know what it is in that person that has been lost. So, when one loses, one is also faced with something enigmatic: something is hiding in the loss, something is lost within the recesses of loss.* Simple searching. Kristin Prevallet writes, *The lack of communication between the living and the dead makes the living wild with fear.*

We cannot communicate with the dead, and yet we must find them in order to bury them.

What a bind.

THERE IS NO SPACE BETWEEN bodies in the room. There is so much space between bodies in the room.

That year Solomon lived in a sunroom off the back end of a house that was partially collapsed. He had never been more popular nor more in the grip of drugs.

It was 2005 and Solomon threw a New Year's Eve party. I remember he walked through the crowd to the stereo and played a song that was our father's favorite. It was unlike any other music played that night. A conspicuous soft-rock interloper in a room of early 2000s R&B. He was offering me something to hold onto in the wilderness of his friends and his life. We no longer knew each other so he gave me something from the past, a common point on the horizon. I saw him offer me something and for the rest of the evening I sat in the front seat of my maroon sedan in the driveway and cried.

IN THE FIRST DARK HOURS of 2008, Solomon and I welcomed the new year in Rome. The kind of celebration that encourages extension. We were alone together in the sea of it. He loved that everyone was shattering empty glass bottles on the street. He loved the chaos. He loved the lawlessness he perceived. He was alive. We slogged back to the hotel covered in the evening. We drank all the champagne in the minibar. We woke up feeling it was the same year stretched over.

I STRAY. FRITZ IS COMING up through all places. Trapped in the kind of time that is smothered by decades. *He just cried and cried.* I look for the small dates between the stories. I stray. Trench rot. The feet are wet for too long. It catches in the hands. A fever. There is no distinction between *enlisted* and *drafted* in the records. I cower. I stray. I highlight references. First there is Indiana.

Fritz writes a letter to Bernice. An aspiration of balance—that these waters are even, that these waters hold. Fritz is dating Agnes when he leaves Indiana. She goes to the farewell party. They all had a farewell party.

My COUSIN SAYS OF HER brother's murder that she had to find a version of the events that she could live with. She welded together pieces of story to protect it from her endless speculation. I watch video of American troops marching into Naples. I am looking everywhere for a version of events I can live with.

First to the Great Lakes, then Camp Wolters, Texas. He would have landed at Salerno sometime in September and so we have a point that is something like still on the field and the point pulls into itself until more points are swirling. Reserve. Replace. Bernice doesn't remember hearing about Salerno. My blood fiction. Maneuver around corrosion and a complex of truth telling. Fritz looks up at the rain and wonders which way is Indiana. Fritz comes down the stairs to his farewell party singing, *I can take the world on.*

We search for an opening in the edge by instinct, repeating our own words like a confused ship's distress call, making a record of the search to come back for, of which to be a part.

HISTORY: A CYCLE THAT IS GRIEVED and made separate so that each time it is some kind of new.

On November 29, 1943, the 45th division were a distraction. General Clark writes home, *Don't worry about the losses.* I make a note to ask Bernice about the funeral service. Back and forth like memorizing a lie. We are attached. It is raining. The fire is high and already out.

The last letter from Fritz arrives in Indiana after the KIA telegram. The letter is dated November 28, 1943. A song from the dead. Fritz's mother finds comfort in knowing he was still writing letters the day before he was killed. Carve out the comfort from the great blank wall of *dying in action.*

In 1949, a box arrives at the Saint James Catholic Cemetery in Indiana. This is a test. To bury may not be to know. *At 0600 on 29 November the 1st Battalion, 179th Infantry began the attack on the right flank but met small-arms, mortar, and artillery fire from the front and right.* Punishment. Open ocean. Fritz is still crying into his sister's stomach. I can hear it. *Replacement, that was what he was.* To move a hillside handful by handful into our stomachs so we can translate the void as architecture.

Come, stand in the center of the sickness. I am unprepared for miles. The Winter Line is less than a two-hour drive from Naples. A birthplace that doesn't let up.

When does one learn how to hold it?

When a saint comes to stir the rain into open ocean.

I make plans to travel to the Winter Line: to find and bury him. A grass-green ambition.

IN EUROPE, I'M UNSURE WHAT I am looking for—who I am looking for. I need to touch the ground where I think Fritz might have been. I could be wrong. It could mean nothing. Solomon is not here.

Before me are the bones of Thomas Aquinas minus his head and right thumb. The body was removed from the ground sometime after burial, his head was separated and boiled. His right thumb is in Milan, his head is in Rome and the rest in a box here in Toulouse. What body is this that finds so much trouble?

I am two points along the trajectory of an arrow, so I am necessarily nowhere and thus, I am dead. It's a cold fear like being too far from the ocean.

The Winter Line is just a two-hour drive from here.

I AM STAYING FIRST IN a house with a friend, making my way slowly to the Winter Line. I may be afraid to reach it and so stretching the days. The caretaker of this house is a man named Fritz L. When he introduces himself to me, I don't know how to tell him I am looking for another Fritz, that I am looking for a ghost. It's Sunday and there is a market. Fritz L. was going to drive us, but he hasn't called. He isn't well.

Instead, I go to a church on the edge of town. I light a candle and say, *Solomon.* The stained-glass windows are impossibly broken. I don't touch the holy water, but I don't break the windows either. I beg silently to be allowed to leave here the parts I can't carry, the parts I will someday come back for because they will fit again inside my body. The door is heavy behind me. I leave my dead inside the stone with a dying candle. The candle must be out by now. I left them in the dark.

Fritz L. coughs, sits heavily at the table and says, *Death is agrèable.* I take my map of the Winter Line and look up a small bed and breakfast nearby. The coming rain is everywhere.

How I need to believe that I did not leave them in the stone with a dying candle—that I did not even think of it.

ON THIS BALCONY, SOFT PURPLE bells have crept in with the green. In this field is some kind of time to believe in. Miracles, I am sorry I have not kept better track of you.

Fritz L. takes us to the market. He can't catch his breath. It rains all day and there is a burst of amnesty. We are saturated by what we are not.

I try to explain: we do not share history. A single scene played over and over against the world, as in empty streets. A choreographed distraction. A division of space into increments of away. A woman tells me, *Let the robins fly through the house.* She tries to find what is vulnerable amid the storm. I wake up missing Solomon from the belly. Fritz writes a letter to Bernice in the rain. Solomon is driving down the mountain road. My mother is searching. Fritz is firing fast. My mother sees the officer come up the driveway to say they have located the vehicle. My mother falls to the ground. My aunt falls to the ground. Solomon tries to free himself from the mud. I fall to the ground. Fritz is cold and wet. Fritz L. has a failing heart. Time is folding into the center in all places. Walking straight up a hill that does not peak.

IN THE SUMMER OF 1941, Bernice is twelve years old. I begin digging as
though the whole beast of it is swimming somewhere. Because to hold
it open like the eyes and speak into it is more dirty glass, more leaping
and asking. This is the field I came to ask for. Count out the steps as
they turn into coal or butter depending on the light. It gets covered in
dust as it comes home and is no longer challenged to exist. There are
saints here. Saints in the water, and the water moves quick.

IT COMES BACK TO THE same stretch of road no matter the distance or wildness. My mother says, *No one loves their children like I do.* A punishment. Open ocean. She believes it. The same stretch of road. There are moments I believe her too. What happens if I find this place? Is it in fact rooted here, reachable? Emptiable?

A KIND OF BIRTHPLACE THAT doesn't let up. The care package sent to Fritz by his mother is returned unopened. The cookies are smashed and the letter sealed. Did her knees buckle when she opened the box to find her futile gesture and not her son?

Aboard a ship floating off the shore of Salerno, the carrier pigeons are let out for a moment and are promptly lost to the idea of a coastline.

Hello Sis,

How's things around there. It's not so hot here right now but I am still o.k. You'd be surprised if you knew what I am doing now but it's nothing to worry about, everything is well taken care of. You write as often as you can because I'll get all the letters...

Take wild. Furlough. General Clark brings his dog to the landing at Salerno. A special exception. General Clark brings his dog to the Italian Campaign. Today I miss Solomon tepid and tedious.

The pigeons are lost to the idea.

THERE WERE SIX THOUSAND PURPLE Hearts brought to Salerno. There were not enough. Fritz L. is too ill to have the heart surgery he needs. The weeks grow and become and unleash. Battling along the hillsides just to slide back into the Winter Line without even the recovery of spring. Each step seems enormous, whole cities between them, cornered but unyielding like the way we wait for one another.

I discover online that Lauren Bacall is eighty-nine years old. Solomon is dead, and Lauren Bacall is still alive. I find this stunning. Fritz L. says, *The water is plenty*, but home is a drought. Solomon would have a Jack and Coke. The way his fingers were too big to play the violin. Bernice begins to go blind after she turns eighty-four. Her mother bakes cookies and mails a care package to the Winter Line.

Fritz L. says, *I would rather drown in wine than water.* Patron saint. He says, *You should write something people want to read.* I think he will die soon. Has death followed me across the ocean?

In 2012, I sit outside on a wooden staircase to make a phone call to say Solomon was found dead on a mountain and all the while he is still walking up and down the stairs past the single moment my body is stalled there. Walk into the room and fall over the edge. Fritz L. has leukemia and a heart condition. His body is retaining fluid and the treatment isn't working. The hillsides are at my door. When what is lost is a way to know.

My mother says *half-German half-hillbilly* and spends the rest of her life believing it.

Fritz L. has a body that is failing. He has difficulty getting in and out of his van. He stops for long fits of coughing that have something to do with his heart. He pulls his hospital bracelet off at the kitchen table and says, *You eat like a rabbit...you should eat the rabbit.* The excess fluid in his body bleeds through the skin and soaks his jeans. He refuses to slow his pace. Somewhere he is strong—but slim comfort. In the afternoon, it rains lazily. I am traveling toward the Winter Line and the whole of it is coming up to meet me. I sink through the white comforter to the stone floor and again through the levels of home and think, *Maybe there is no ghost here, no ungodly weather.*

Which way is Indiana from here? I am coming to search but I have to climb over the hillsides at my doorstep. Handful by handful. A plane is shot down and my mother says, *It would be better to die instantly in the air.*

Sometimes I believe her. Sometimes I would like enough time to hold someone's hand.

I ARRIVE AT THE WINTER Line. I drive the winding hills with a map of the movements of the 45th division looking for ghosts and answers and the place where time folds and can be unfolded. I stand in Venafro and hold my breath.

Great-Uncle, I am here but I cannot see you. Your sister sent me. Is this the site of your fear or is it that field over there? Can you tell me if you are still in the water, still writing the letter, still struggling to breathe?

In the bed and breakfast, I'm startled awake in the middle of the night by the sound of cannons. This summer evening has broken into fighting and the thunder is rolling over the hillsides. Monte Cassino is backlit with flashes of lightning gunfire. The rain is pounding at the window. This is the hillside I have come to search. We are bold against the edges tightly.

I NEED TO TELL THOSE out there clinging to the line that they must learn to swim—they will never find a position to hold. Bury my dead with me. The dark clouds move between peaks and they remember an army too. I open the window and the room fills with water. Miracles are broken. My blood fiction. My band of dead come to me with the water and I can hear them struggling. I have never seen it rain before. *Anything to know.* They are still there, cold and wet. Time cracks open just enough for me to see them, but they are too distracted to see me hunkered down in this room in this field in this fissure.

I take a small fennel flower, a relic of each dead and dying and soon to die, and go home covered in dust.

carrion

Polyneikes is to lie unwept and unburied sweet sorry meat for the little lusts of birds.

—Anne Carson, *Antigonick*

THIS IS HOW THE ARGUMENT GOES: They are dead and so they are buried.

This argument can be won and lost.

AFTER HER HOME IS REMODELED, my aunt spends a week in the hospital after she refuses to do much other than lay on the floor in the hallway in the shape Tanner took when he died. She wants to talk to her son, and it's the best place she can think of to speak from. The plywood had been replaced with faux wood flooring and the walls repainted but there is still the distinct fear of falling in that we had felt that first day back inside.

Eventually, my aunt will sell the house, unable to live among the history. Nearly a decade later, the new owner will claim that Tanner is still lingering in the home. He moves items around or makes small sounds and while she has not been particularly bothered, she is worried about him continuing to live in the house as he is quite angry about his death and it would be healthier for him to find everlasting comfort by moving on toward whatever comes next.

Four years after the trial concludes, a woman will recount to a reporter her experience of talking on the phone with her fiancé in the Washington State Penitentiary when Justin Crenshaw suddenly stabbed him in the neck. Her fiancé survives a total of six stab wounds to his neck and face.

AT SENTENCING THE JUDGE TOLD Justin, *I think you are a dangerous person, and I don't say that with animosity or hatred.* She calls him *damaged.* Justin Crenshaw was twenty-two years old when he received two consecutive life sentences for murder. For most people, the story that starts with Justin Crenshaw ends with what amounts to a shrug. Yet he still exists within a system ill-equipped to investigate or understand him. A system in which he walks around a living ghost with no one trying to communicate.

PEOPLE KEEP GETTING SCOOPED OUT of our family one way or another.

I don't know why it matters except to say that it should add up to something.

Shouldn't it?

LET US BURY WITH THE SAME RESOLVE we have when we are screaming.

After Solomon is located, I fly home and find my mother in her driveway with the same torn-down look she had eight years earlier after my father died. Now her son. My mother knows how to fall. This time she sits in a lawn chair outside. She is afraid of her house, of his things, of her life. She no longer has the energy to have a body, so it flops around uselessly.

My mother insists immediately that no one is to see the body. *Solomon is private.* Friends and family visit the funeral home and they are not allowed into the room. His girlfriend goes to the funeral home and she is not allowed into the room. They call repeatedly. He is cremated within the week. Something she didn't want seen. Something she didn't want to learn. Absence as protection. Bury as though it will disappear.

ONCE WHILE DISCUSSING TANNER'S BURIAL, Solomon casually committed this direction:

If I die, put my ashes in a smoothie and drink it. I want all my friends to have some.

We decide to follow his instructions exactly.

To exceed the reasonable.

IN THE MIDDLE OF THE night, my mother calls to tell me she can't. She is half. She is missing half of herself. I shift the weight in order to accommodate more. She tells me she has found a healer. She will find many healers, mediums, spirit guides. My mother calls me late in the night to say she cannot hold it. I take the pieces I can from her. There is no way to say I don't believe that her healer can speak to my dead because I don't know where I'm going either.

My mother refused to let my brother be seen in his death state, refused to have his body be exposed as dead even to herself. To see the body without the brightness behind the eyes, without the warmth of his being in the world, was too painful and instead she chose to swiftly let the body go. I understand this impulse. The dead body is everything and nothing. It is a transitional canvas that readies the mourners for a new world.

Also, I think my mother refused to let anyone see my brother's dead body because she was dragged out of bed to dance on a table. And so, Solomon was born hiding and as a child he would refuse to be naked and was easily embarrassed. I think she was protecting him from being the spectacle she never could shake out of herself.

I tell her to remember that we move through it.

Sometimes with great effort—but remember that we do.

MY BROTHER RETURNS IN A brass box delivered to Stoller's Mortuary. The local funeral home is next to the library which is next to the bank which are together most of downtown Raymond. Inside is all the cabernet-colored carpet and heavy oak furniture one would expect of a small-town mortuary. The woman behind the desk went to high school with my mother and my aunt. She is kind but hosts a necessary detachment from your pain. It's a distance that feels pronounced but understandable when your puffy eyes are in front of her still wild with shock. It was too quiet and so warm I was afraid I was going to melt.

WORD SPREADS THROUGH THE FAMILY that we are going to follow my brother's instructions. We decide it will be a small ceremony separate from the funeral as not everyone will be comfortable participating. We subtly size up each person's openness by mentioning the idea in passing, ready to laugh if they look worried. The majority of his friends and family feel it is a fitting sendoff. White folding chairs are set up in lines in the front yard of Bernice's home on the river. After the service I walk to the water. His friends in stiff borrowed suits and dogs barking. As the crowd of acquaintances thins, a core group lingers because they have heard we are planning to have a ceremony with extreme edges. Arrangements are made for a collection of blenders and juices to be waiting for us at a neighboring house.

When the time comes to perform our secondary service, no one is sure how to begin. We look at each other bleary-eyed and defeated. My cousin gathers her reserve of gumption and opens the small urn, dips her finger inside and licks it. Everyone takes a breath. She smiles and says, *Not bad.* Everyone relaxes. *Solomon, you taste…* There are three batches to accommodate the nearly forty people. Small paper cups are passed out and everyone raises and then tips them into their mouths together. Some is spilled in the process, spilled pink with small gray crumbs. I pick up a grey pebble and hold it in my hand… *like raspberries and outrageousness.* Bury with intent.

WHERE WE COME FROM is taken from us and returned as some kind of scattering, some kind of motion we do not recognize. We mix a portion of the remaining ashes with ink and tattoo ourselves to make him seem permanent, to make ourselves feel saturated.

I BURY THE DEAD in my body when there is nowhere else to bury them.

Are all dead buried in the body? Whose dead are buried in which body?

My mother does not know where to scatter the remaining ashes. That summer day on the front porch when he requested the grand communal act, he did not specify about the excess.

To be buried is to be torn apart.

She decides to keep them.

It's Solomon's thirtieth birthday. He has been dead for seven years. I am thinking about a dream I had in which my mother and I tried to find my brother in a wildfire. Our neighborhood was overtaken by the flames and when we reached our house, we found him there dead and burned. I am thinking about finding him there and the feeling in my stomach that we abandoned him to death. That he is alone because we could not keep him in the world. I am thinking what a beautiful system it is that our bodies rot and fall apart and decay into the earth. How human it is that we try to find ways to thwart this.

When the reality of death and mourning is too tangled and overgrown, I turn to the body. I whisper, *Happy birthday brother* as I walk through Mountain View Cemetery in Oakland. It's a drizzling day. I see a gravestone for a Solomon and wonder if we can share. The cemetery is so alive. It is alive in a way that does not mock the dead nor all the things his dead body cannot do but serves instead as a gentle reminder of what must be shared.

I was not a great sister. I think I am a better sister to his dead body. The dead are on my side and I am on the side of the dead.

I AM DRINKING A NICE bottle of wine that an ex bought me called Richard the Lion-Heart because it's my dead brother's birthday and I don't want to be a person who doesn't have the nice thing and instead saves it for some perfect occasion that will never come.

I am having the wine and thinking about the Donner Party and survival cannibalism. My friend says, *Cannibalism freaks me out.* They say it as though they're speaking of some unique revulsion. I play along and ask, *Why does cannibalism freak you out?* They explain that it freaks them out because they think it is plausible that people will eat people much more often in the future, that we are much too comfortable not knowing what is in our food. Then they say, *Also I am afraid of being eaten.* I think this is closer to the truth. When we say that eating the flesh of the dead is against some natural or spiritual law, are we really just saying that we are afraid to be eaten?

Or is it that we cannot stop seeing life in the faces of the dead? I suspect that we do not only see the life of the individual in the face of the dead, but our own faces and our own mortality and somehow to desecrate what is left there (in this most classic of traumatic ways) makes us see that the body is a temporary companion of flesh and blood and not fixed to ourselves in the way we would like.

Unless, of course, your body rots below you with your eyes still open. You may then find yourself in need of a graceful separation; a new and welcome bodyless state. You may find that you see yourself instead in the faces of those able to do all the things you once did and find death in your own.

My MOTHER WASN'T AT THE HOSPITAL for the final round of tortured waiting for her ex-husband to die. There had been so many emergency trips that she couldn't fully believe it was the last one. Or maybe she knew she wouldn't be able to stand in the room and then walk out. As my brother and I drove up the driveway after, we saw her collapsed outside the front door. She looked like a marionette when the strings are dropped, jointless and wrapped around our Golden Retriever. She only truly swallowed the death when she saw our faces. I wanted to apologize for bringing it home. I wanted to chastise her for not being strong enough to stand for it.

My father returned in a small cardboard box.

The cremated remains of Michael E. Davis.

My father had time for instructions. He knew his body was failing. The conversations are clear and exacting. His ashes are to be spread at the base of a great cedar tree in the forest. *Yes, this one.* He likes the wholeness of it, to be absorbed into the root structure. These are the stories we hold. A small portion of the ashes are placed in a silver necklace. A portion is set aside in a miniature urn for me to keep. This is how I bury my dead: carefully portioned.

To bury there must be a searching and there must be a finding. The box lived on the top shelf of our kitchen cabinet for over a year. When we finally found the right weekend, his mother sent along a bag of rose petals and we set out to follow his instructions. As we passed the sign for the Quinault Rainforest, we realized somehow for the first time that we were looking for a specific tree in a forest.

Someone called to the cardboard box on the backseat, *Mike, which tree?* Everyone laughed.

SCATTERING IS INDELICATE AND IMPRECISE. It inevitably lacks the pageantry one hopes for. Inside the cardboard box is a clear plastic bag. The grey dust is mostly smooth but littered with white pieces large enough to be curious about. The grey body gets everywhere, coming back up with the wind before settling in a wide disappearing path around the trunk of the tree. After it is finished, we stand for a moment in silence wondering what is appropriate. We feel that we have accomplished something but there has been no announcement of a ceremony completed, no music swelling, not even a sense that anything has changed.

On our way back to the car we pass a young couple. We have soft grey beneath our fingernails. Mourning pulled back from an edge it has created; pulled back and put on display. Grief is obscene.

I have not yet returned to the tree. I am not sure I could find it again. I like to believe I could. I like to believe it matters.

Lauren Bacall dies, and Fritz L. succumbs to his heart condition the next day.

Patron saint.

Tanner's body was released by police shortly after the autopsy was completed and after each of his injuries had been methodically recorded. His body then arrived at the funeral home where he was embalmed and prepared for an open casket viewing. At the funeral home, his mother and siblings visited the body. They combed his hair, sat and talked with him as he appeared stiff and pale but otherwise restful. The body that had held so much of their lives was now hollow but nevertheless familiar enough to be difficult to leave alone in such a cold room.

TANNER HAD LONG SINCE LEFT the Mormon church, but still, there was a lavish casserole-filled Mormon funeral attended by some four hundred people. There was a large screen projecting a slideshow of pictures from his life: summer vacations, friends, prom, family reunions, baby pictures, showing-off pictures, candid pictures. There were tables and tables of mayonnaise-laden side dishes. His father made a speech that went on too long because he needed it to keep going and everyone understood. His uncle spoke at length about the wonderful qualities of the nephew he hardly knew and awkwardly shamed his five- and six-year-old children in the second row for not being more like the cousin they couldn't remember having met. There were pallbearers and an open casket.

AFTER THE FUNERAL, THE COFFIN was sealed and readied for transport to a small country cemetery in southwestern Washington. A caravan of vehicles accompanied the coffin for the six-hour drive from Spokane to Raymond. His father and brothers helped the funeral attendants lift the coffin into the back of an SUV and we set out on our last trip with Tanner.

Halfway to the other side of the state, the caravan pulled off at a rest stop. Everyone was hungry and weathered from the incessant process of it all. Standing in a somber circle, no one seemed to know the appropriate way to travel in this context. We decided we should eat but Tanner's brother said, *We can't all go have lunch and leave Tanner in the car.* It was true, and everyone believed it. Instead we purchased snacks from the vending machines. A picture was taken of the group half smiling and posing together. A field trip of grief.

TANNER'S HEADSTONE IS GRANITE WITH engraved music notes and an oval picture of him from prom in a black suit smiling under a wide-brimmed fedora. If you are standing on top of him, you can see almost nothing aside from green hilltops layered forever along the horizon. When we were children, we walked to this cemetery from our grandmother's home during summer vacations. This was our place of adventure. Between Bernice's home and the cemetery is a long and winding road with trees overhanging both sides making a tunnel through the forest. It's a damp and earnest place to be a child. We strolled through the cemetery, communing with ghosts and solving mysteries. We must have walked past where Tanner would be buried. I wonder if there was a shiver when time folded in half there. I wonder if he liked the view or hardly noticed.

TANNER WAS BURIED IN A town he never lived in but one he certainly came from. On my last visit to the cemetery, my dog jumped out of the car and promptly peed on the corner of Tanner's ornate headstone. I looked around embarrassed before remembering that the person below me wasn't a stranger. He would have enjoyed the dog's inability to be reverent.

My aunt was told by a cemetery director that burial six feet under is a myth. *People are buried much closer to the surface to save time and money,* he said. She had planned to climb the hill at night and bury the ashes of Tanner's beloved dog Norman above his coffin. She decided against it.

We are unburied as we are buried for the first time. We are dug up and opened. We are held together by distance, softly so that we can imagine we are not separate at all.

WILBUR IS DYING SO MY mother and my aunt fly to Kentucky. They aren't sure why they are going but they need a place to put their thorny attachment to him and maybe he can just take it with him when he goes. They find him gray and sweetened to the point of rot.

The sisters agree to watch over their father for the afternoon. He needs to use the bathroom. The girls stare at one another. There is no precedent for this. No real history of touch. They try to help him into the bathroom, but he can't quite make it and hot sick urine dampens his jeans. The old man chuckles, *Well a little dab'll do ya.* It comes from the same vein of charm in him that made it not so bad to be what they were.

The family Wilbur made after he left Bernice adores him. He reinvented himself much softer. His eldest daughters—as well as their pain and anger—are not welcome. When he dies, they will stand in the corner stifling their laughter as his younger children wail at his bedside.

The relic of which man?

WE ARE ALWAYS WAITING TO be buried or unburied depending on the time of day.

Tanner shares the small cemetery in Raymond with a local legend. In 1855, nineteen-year-old Willie Kiel wanted so much to travel from his home in Missouri to the green promised land of Washington that when he died of malaria before completing the journey, his father sealed him in his coffin with 100-proof Golden Rule whiskey to preserve him until they reached their destination. His family buried him on the Willapa River before determining the climate to be too damp for their liking and moving south, leaving Willie's body a strange leftover token of forced and symbolic accomplishment. His headstone is fenced off at the top of a small hill, an example of a deep refusal to sever from the dead. I picture the person who opened the barrel, pulled out the long-dead body of a nineteen-year-old boy and buried him on a remote hillside. I like to imagine it helped someone, even slightly.

But in death, we do not find company. We do not accompany. The bar across the street is a converted trailer. It's called Tombstone Willy's.

THERE IS LITTLE CERTAIN about how and when the dead were eaten by
the Donner Party. They spent months snowed into the Sierra Nevada
mountains with nothing to eat. They ate a thick glue made from the
hides of the oxen they used to cover the roofs of their shelters. They
boiled their leather shoelaces. When does one's physical reality force
out the sense that the dead still have needs? How many days before
there is hardly room left in one's brain for the thought that the dead are
sacred and untouchable? How many days would it take me?

I bury the bodies where I can. There is no plan. There is never a
plan but if I am ever trapped with you on a snowy mountainside, boil
my body into a thick glue and eat it.

I drank the pink and grey swirl from the wax-paper Dixie cup
standing on the riverbank and rolling the small grey pebble between
my fingers and wondering what of Solomon I have wasted and what I
am taking with me. I am grateful for whatever I consumed, every flake.

THE WOMAN AT THE FUNERAL HOME advises my aunt that Tanner's casket should not be opened before burial. It has been over a week since Tanner's death and even though embalmed, the body has begun to decompose. My aunt listens and nods her head. The following day, before his body is lowered into the earth, she insists that the casket is unsealed and opened one last time.

IN HER 1963 CLASSIC, *THE American Way of Death,* Jessica Mitford describes embalming and restorative art as *so universally employed in the United States and Canada that for years the funeral director did it routinely, without consulting corpse or kin...* She explains that *no law requires embalming, no religious doctrine commends it, nor is it dictated by consideration of health, sanitation, or even of personal daintiness. In no part of the world but in North America is it widely used.*

Tanner's possible wishes were discussed often in the days and weeks after his death. Most of us remember having had a conversation with him about what he would want but no one remembers the conversations accurately enough. Most healthy twenty-year-olds don't bother to think about what they would want, let alone make their preferences known. Few close to Tanner believe he would have wanted to be embalmed and buried, but in the stunned aftermath no one put up much of a fight. His parents believe in both heaven and the body. No one believed that he would stay preserved under the ground and yet it was of critical importance that he look as though he could wake up at any moment as he was lowered into the dirt. His eyes were sewn shut. His blood was removed and replaced. His many wounds were filled and covered as though we could erase the knife, as though we could erase the time.

In my last conversation with Tanner, we discussed our imagined deaths but the details available to me have been slipping away for years. I don't believe he wanted to be embalmed or buried, and so I must ask: What does it mean to be buried wrong? Is it the same as or different than being trapped?

YOU CANNOT TIE ME TO your delicate perception of the dead body. You cannot convince me that my dead linger there. You cannot convince me that their eyes being sewn shut shares a vocabulary with sleep or that the performance of their face is more relevant than their liver or lungs which were unceremoniously discarded.

DETAILS ARRIVE TO MY INBOX one year after my request. The Individual Deceased Personnel File for Fritz Relleke. An infestation of likely: *KIA - shell frag. rt. leg.*

It is all there. The details of his body laid out. All of the correspondence between Bernice's parents and the US government after the war is documented and saved, including their request to have the body returned to them.

The Burial Report, which is included in the PDF emailed to me by the US government, is a document written onsite—something that happened on the hillside by whomever was near enough to complete it. The detailed instructions given for battlefield burial are included as well.

The bureaucratic confusion is immediately apparent. Relleke is misspelled on the Burial Report and the ID tag does not have A as his middle initial. The date of death is listed as thirteen days before he wrote his last letter. It is listed as his birthday. This is clearly a mistake. All documents after Jan 1 list the date of death as November 29, 1943. The name of the person buried to his left is scratched out and rewritten because his first and last names have been confused for each other. After repeated correspondence, it is decided that these are indeed the correct remains and they should be sent home to Indiana.

The ID tag buried with the body is taped to the back of the form after the exhumation. The form and the ID tag are photocopied. It appears partially melted.

I TELL BERNICE THAT THE body she buried in Indiana was in fact the body of her brother. She has always wondered about this. I can tell her *shell fragments in the right leg.* Bernice is grateful to know more after so many years with just her imagination. I can tell her the day he died and the city he died in. I can tell her I traveled to that city, and that I saw him there on the hillside. I can tell her he isn't so far away anymore. I can tell her he is not missing.

She says quietly that she is the last person living to have ever known her brother. This struck her recently and she can't stop thinking about it. She is turning ninety-three this December. I think she means hers will be his real death.

WHEN TANNER DIED, MORMONISM TOOK care of it. There were few decisions to be made other than choosing a coffin color and headstone image.

When Solomon died, there was a sudden contending with our nuclear family's rejection of custom and religion. A vacuum left by the lack of church—no foundation on which to start the process of detangling our lives from Solomon's. Death customs based in religious community and tradition hold up their followers in times of grief when they can hardly open their eyes to face living without. In a secular context, how do we fill this gap of ceremony? Custom and ritual, clarity and certainty: the little comforts when everything prickles.

TOWARD THE VERY END OF his life, my father dutifully tried on each religion as one test drives a car before committing. He did it with a touch of irony, a lot of curiosity, and overwhelming fear. There was all this time to see death coming. So much time without the gentle fiction of immortality so many of us unconsciously tell ourselves every day.

When he died, there was a small gathering that if it had a name would be called a Secular Northwest Memorial. Friends and family gathered at his home, ate from cheese and vegetable plates in black tops and jeans. We had a guestbook and I made a playlist of his favorite music. We mingled surrounded by all of his things exactly as he had left them. His clothes still on hangers in the bedroom. Amy's Organic dinners still in the freezer. I wandered around in the backyard with a small paper plate of carrot sticks. I smiled at each guest who didn't know what to say to me. I invited just a couple friends from high school, most of whom had never encountered death outside of movies and looked at me pitifully. I walked into the bathroom and put my face to the black and white tile floor and sobbed until someone knocked needing to use the bathroom. I don't remember what I wore. I don't remember what Solomon wore or said. I remember the cool tile of the bathroom floor. A grounding.

Solomon had no spiritual leanings. He was a twenty-three-year-old kid. My family went to a Universalist Church once or twice but decided we had simply too much to do on the weekends. My mother and father always noted that there are lots of belief systems and that one day I might even pick one. This seemed reasonable enough. I have always been grateful for the way it allowed me to look at various religions as equally well-told stories. But what it means to be held by one of these systems—to grow into and out of it—was completely lost on me. And so, at twenty-five, I was utterly unable to decide what should be done. There was no story under me, no ground.

When Solomon died, the name for the type of service would be Makeshift Riverside Devastation Picnic. We had no answers to any of the questions. Where should we have the service? A church wasn't appropriate. To me a town-hall, baseball field, or supermarket would have each sounded equally sensical because the answer was emphatically *nowhere*. There should be no service. He should not—cannot—be dead. This thought must be the most common post-tragedy hang-up but without ritual to rely on, it threatened to derail us. Of course, decisions had to be made soon—within days or weeks—well before one can remember to brush their own teeth, let alone plan an event.

THE DAY AFTER MY BROTHER's body was found, my mother packed a suitcase and drove from Portland back to her childhood home in Raymond. I don't think it was a decision. I think it was her nervous system demanding retreat. It was her body adjusting to holding his inside her sternum. We found ourselves on the small front lawn in front of Bernice's home on the river with enough spaghetti to feed everyone. Garlic bread and an a cappella rendition of "Yellow Submarine" by two of my uncles.

The ceremony—too strong a word for that afternoon—was followed by our other, more private ritual. One that felt particular and beautiful. One that actually did feel strong. We buried him in our bodies because there was no one to tell us what to do.

THE DEAD DECAY IN MY body. Sometimes I feel a little jolt in my brain—a short circuit, a charge, a fraction. I blink and there is a buzz and then it's gone and something is gone with it. I keep my dead there and little pieces leak out. Sometimes my left ear rings suddenly as though just my left side is in an airplane climbing to a new altitude. It is the dead blocking the way. My eyes are blue in much the same tone as my mother's and my father's but not blue like my brother's which made him look inhuman, sparkling like a mineral. I think he kept his dead in his eyes. The skin under my eyes sags a little more each year. So does my mother's. I wonder if my father would have had sagging eye skin if he had lived longer. My wrists can only take light work and need constant breaks and stretches. Otherwise the dead creep into the tendons and constrict up to my shoulders. The migraines come when the dead are angry—as though my head is their haunted house and they are trapped in there moaning and growling and rattling the engine. I wonder who I will haunt with such gusto. I would like to apologize in advance for my remnants. I don't mean to keep you up at night.

THE SAME CHRISTMAS THAT A flood destroys the double-wide trailer that is the bar called Tombstone Willy's, Solomon's dog dies. Or rather, we kill Solomon's dog—the mercy. It's 2019 and we discover he is in kidney failure after we rush him to the vet clinic. I'm not wearing socks. There is no time. We think we are going to bring him home with fluids and antibiotics, but we bring him home swaddled in one of the used sheets from the thrift store that the vet keeps on hand for this kind of situation.

After my brother died, his dog was his proxy in the world. After seven years, the dog could no longer stand up on his own. His back legs were tired. His stomach was tired. He wouldn't eat. I watched fog in the valley tracing back toward a beginning. I could see the small town stalked by grey as it holds the river risen to flood and the black green forest behind it. The rotting wood of empty storefronts and crumbling houses reflected into creamy watercolors on the surface of the riverbend. For years, my mother would hold the face of this dog and know it was the same face her son held. A life stretched over by association. His flopping pink white ears, *like galloping angel wings*, she often noted. Just for the night, we put the swaddled bundle of familiar muscle in the room where my mother keeps Solomon's things. It never feels right to leave the body of a loved one in the car. Traditions of intuition.

IN THE MORNING, MY MOTHER insists we uncover the dog's head, so she can put his Christmas scarf around his neck. She wraps his cold body in the heavy winter coat my brother left hanging in his closet. He should take with him something of value. It is the time for dying everywhere. We dig a large hole in the yard and slowly lower the wrapped package. As we feed dirt back over the top, the package shifts and settles, finds home. My mother puts a handful of calendula to seed over where we have left him in the earth. My mother cries because she hates that he is in the rain. I find that I am glad he has the coat. The rotting bothers me but it's the crisp severing that shakes me—the way he opened his eyes to the sound of his name in one minute and the water is soaking into the loose dirt above his unfeeling body the next. Just as he was severed from my brother. As we are all severed. How easily we succumb to death. How small we are in the face of it. It is the time for dying everywhere. But I feel left again in the wake, still breathing.

instructions for burial

PREPARATION OF BODY: Have body examined by member of Medical Department whenever possible (to attach E.M.T. Form 52b). Remove all personal property: remove one identification tag, leave other on body in protected position (in case of enemy dead, leave 1/2 tag on body, forward 1/2 with personal effects). If no tag present make notation of identifying data on form, protect in sealed bottle, canteen, spent shell or best available container, and bury with remains. If unidentified, take fingerprints of both hands; if this is not possible fill out tooth-chart and note height, weight, color of eyes and hair, tattoo marks, birthmarks, etc. and other data as serial no. of weapon, laundry marks, where body found, etc. Wrap body in shelter half, mattress cover, or blanket when available.

BURIAL: Dig grave to a depth of five feet (hasty battlefield burials, to sufficient depth to prevent elements from exposing the body). Place only one body in a grave. Dig graves side by side, row behind row.

MARKING OF GRAVE: Fasten identification tag to temporary name peg and place at head of grave. For enemy dead, write data on peg. When pegs are not available, copy data on a piece of paper, place in bottle, spent shell, or other receptacle, seal tightly and place so as to mark and identify grave. If identification tag cannot be fastened to peg or placed in container, do not leave at grave but forward with report of burial. If only one tag is found on body, it should be buried with body. The information thereon should be written on marker or placed in container at head of grave. Do not use weapons or helmets to mark graves.